Life With The Baoulé

by Vincent Guerry

Translation by Nora Hodges

Introduction by Richard Horovitz

3CP Three Continents Press

First English Edition:

Three Continents Press
4201 Cathedral Ave., N.W.
Washington, D.C. 20016

© Three Continents Press 1975

Life with the Baoulé was originally published in French in
Abidjan, Ivory Coast, by I.N.A.D.E.S., in 1972, as *La Vie
quotidienne dans un village Baoulé.*

ISBN 0-914478-15-X (Hard)
ISBN 0-914478-16-8 (Soft)

Library of Congress Catalog Number: 75-15876

CIP

Library of Congress Cataloging in Publication Data

Front cover by Patty Zukerowski.
(Cover is based on wooden urn used by Baoulé diviners: mice were
placed in the urn atop carefully arranged sticks. After being allowed to
scramble about, the mice were removed, and the diviners carefully
"read" the oracle in the tumbled straw.)

Photographs courtesy Benedict Tisa (Men Dancing, Baoulé Girls, and
Five Boys) and I.N.A.D.E.S. (Woman Bathing Baby, Man Weaving,
Women Cooking Foutou, Women Spinning, Baoulé Compound, Baoulé
Chiefs at Meeting).

Life With The Baoulé

Table of Contents

Introduction

The modern day West African nation of Ivory Coast boasts over sixty different ethnic groups, although its population is a modest 4.5 million. One of these groups is the Baoulé, who number 765,000, and whose culture forms the subject of this book. These introductory remarks are designed first to provide an historical background, and second to analyze within a broader anthropological framework some of the author's specific observations on the Baoulé, who still remain virtually unknown to the American reader. More familiar perhaps are the medieval empires of Ghana and Mali which have lent their names to two other modern West African nations.

The wealth of those ancient kingdoms was legendary. In 1324 the Malian king, Mansa Kankan Musa, spent so much gold in Cairo on his way to Mecca that its value fell and prices rose in the Egyptian economy. This great wealth enabled the Malian rulers to lure the most advanced scholars, doctors, and holy men of the then-flourishing Muslim world to urban centers like Timbuktu. There mosques and universities were constructed out of the desert sands by al-Saheli, an architect from Moorish Granada. While much of the gold which formed the basis of their wealth came from the Bambuk-Bure region of what is today Senegal, the ancient Malians were constantly on the alert for new sources of the precious metal.

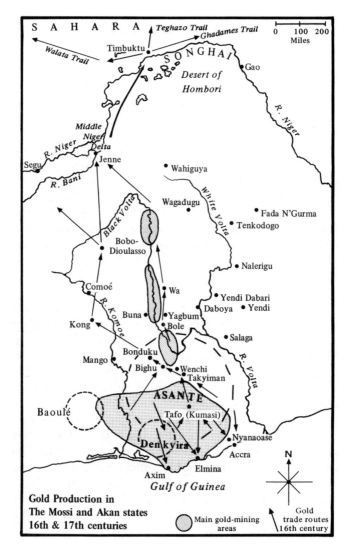

S A H A R A *Teghazo Trail*
Ghadames Trail
0   100   200
Miles
Walata Trail
Timbuktu
S O N G H A I
Gao
Desert of Hombori
R. Niger
Middle Niger Delta
R. Niger
Segu
Jenne
R. Bani
• Wahiguya
White Volta
Wagadugu
• Fada N'Gurma
Tenkodogo
Black Volta
Bobo-Dioulasso
• Nalerigu
Comoé
• Wa
R. Komoé
Buna •
Yagbum
Bole
Yendi Dabari
Daboya • Yendi
Kong
• Salaga
R. Volta
Mango
Bonduku
Bighu
Wenchi
Takyiman
Baoulé
ASANTE
Tafo (Kumasi)
Denkyira
Nyanaoase
Accra
Axim
Elmina
Gulf of Guinea
N

**Gold Production in
The Mossi and Akan states
16th & 17th centuries**

Main gold-mining areas

Gold trade routes 16th century

The large auriferous deposits located between the Volta and Comoé rivers in the zone of ecological transition from savannah to forest therefore began to attract Malian traders southwards as early as mid-fifteenth century. About the same time Prince Henry's Portuguese navigators were drawn along the West African coast towards the same sources of wealth. In 1482 they built the first European fort in the tropics at Elmina ("the mine") with hopes of exporting as much gold as possible. Partly in response to both Malian and Portuguese stimuli several interior kingdoms grew up in the forested area in the vicinity of the gold reserves, the best known being Asante [Ashanti], from whom the Baoulé are generally considered to be an offshoot.

Recent scholars believe that the ancestors of the Asante used the capital generated by gold mining to purchase captives from further north, whom they used to clear the dense tropical forests. They gradually created farms, cultivating tuberous yams, cassava, and other staple food crops. Socially they were organized into exogamous matriclans, with inheritance being passed through female members. Toward the end of the seventeenth century certain of these matriclans gained supremacy over the others by the use of firearms imported from the coast. Their leader, Osei Tutu, is credited with the founding of the Asante kingdom. He conquered and pacified the people around Kumase* (located in the center of modern Ghana), where he established his capital. Then, in 1701, the Asante defeated the Denkyira, who had been their former overlords and the most powerful kingdom between Asante and the sea.

* Or, Kumasi.

Osei Tutu used allegiance to the Golden Stool and a variety of other symbols to unify the Asante politically. However, this period of conquest and consolidation on the part of Asante also aggravated certain fissiparous tendencies. Some of the peoples who had been tributary to Denkyira took advantage of its defeat to flee to the west, and thus avoided becoming subjects of Asante, Denkyira's successor, or falling victim to the Atlantic slave trade. Many of these emigrants, including some Denkyira themselves, moved into what is today central Ivory Coast and gradually introduced such diverse elements as yam cultivation and matrilineal descent patterns.

According to Baoulé traditions a major migration took place following the death of Osei Tutu. A succession crisis broke out in Kumase between two claimants to the Asante throne, Opoku Ware, who eventually became king, and Dako, who lost both his bid for power and his life. Dako's sister, Aura Poku, fearing reprisals from the victorious faction, gathered her brother's partisans together and fled westward from Kumase towards the Comoé River.

Baoulé legends recount that Queen Poku and her followers were indeed pursued right to the banks of the Comoé, which they were unable to cross due to its turbulence. The Sorcerers* of the group solemnly proclaimed that the gods of the water would be appeased only when the group's most cherished

---

*Finding connotation-free English renderings for important Baoulé concepts like fetish and sorcery is not easy. It greatly troubled the translator of this volume, and plagues all those concerned with adequately conveying ideas from one culture to another.

possession was sacrificed to them. The women immediately threw all of their golden adornments—rings, bracelets and earrings—into the surging waters, but to no avail. Finally it became apparent that the ultimate offering had to be human, but no member of the group appeared willing to give up the life of his child. It was then that the queen, who was also a mother, lifted her baby, her only son, high above her head and threw him into the raging river. Miraculously a bridge of hippopotamuses appeared, and upon their backs the people were able to cross to safety. Once on the far bank they prostrated themselves in graditude before Aura Poku, their queen. But the queen, being also a mother, could only enunciate one word through her tears: *ba-o-li,* "the child is dead."

From this experience, claim the Baoulé, they derived not only their name and consciousness as a distinct group, but also the importance of matrilineal descent. It is now assumed that a relatively small number of culture carriers introduced innovations over the course of a century or two, and that a new society grew up in the central Ivory Coast which combined and modified both pre-existing and intrusive elements. Anthropologists, for instance, today consider Baoulé kinship patterns to be cognatic, although the Baoulé still think of themselves as matrilineal. While the migration legend may have telescoped certain historic events, giving the impression of a large number of people moving at once rather than the gradual introduction of new cultural elements, it served a political function as well. The Queen Poku story became a myth which provided a sense of unity and identity during the process of assimilation and integration.

Those who became known as Baoulé peoples over the century and a half following the initial migrations remained primarily agriculturalists. They cleared, planted and harvested in a routine which differed little from those times to the current ways described in Vincent Guerry's *Life with the Baoulé*. In addition the Baoulé hunted, and mined gold, which they traded with their African neighbors, although not on any large scale. They also worked the gold (and wood) into a variety of ceremonial and decorative objects in a style which appeared particularly pleasing to the earliest western observers who found its "refinement" closer to their canons of beauty than much of the art they encountered on the African continent.

Politically the Baoulé remained fragmented. They did not go on to create a centralized or bureaucratized kingdom in the eighteenth and nineteenth centuries as did the Asante, but rather developed a complex series of kinship alliances. This lack of political centralization was most irksome to the French who endeavored to colonize the Baoulé in the early years of the twentieth century, since it meant that there was no one Baoulé king whom they could win over and thereby co-opt his people, nor was there any one leader whom they could crush dramatically. While France had already maintained treaties and commercial relations with various coastal peoples for half a century prior to the establishment of the Ivory Coast Colony in 1893, most of the Baoulé of the interior had never even seen a European until the twentieth century. They resisted what the French euphemistically termed "pacification" with guerilla warfare, for which they were eminently suited, given their superior knowledge of the bush.

It was only the technological superiority of the West (primarily the Maxim gun) which enabled the French to subdue the Baoulé during the opening decades of the twentieth century. Since then their outward existence has changed little by little. The Baoulé despised the occasional *corvées* imposed upon them, such as working on road maintenance. They disliked equally having to pay taxes, which forced them to earn European money, previously unknown to their self-sustaining economy. To do so many began planting the "cash crops" introduced by the Europeans, primarily coffee. Here, too, Africans were at a disadvantage, since Europeans received preferential prices for their coffee, and often commandeered forced African labor as well.

It was not until the inter-war years that an articulate Baoulé spokesman emerged to voice these grievances. Félix Houphouët was the nephew (more important than a son in a matrilineal society) of the chief of a major Baoulé sub-group, and had been educated as a doctor in Dakar, then the administrative capital of French West Africa. In 1944 Houphouët founded the African Planters' Union *(Syndicat Agricole Africain)* to protest the unequal conditions and demand that African planters receive the same advantages as their French counterparts. With the approval of the French, Houphouët transformed the African Planters' Union into the Democratic Party of Ivory Coast *(Parti Démocratique de Côte d'Ivoire)* two years later.

After his first electoral victory in French colonial politics, Houphouët added "Boigny"—which means a ram and signifies an invincible force in Baoulé—to his name. His party prospered despite several initial difficulties, including rivalries between ethnic groups within the territory the French had delimited and called the Ivory Coast. Other peoples, notably those closer to the coast who had been in contact with Europeans and western education longer than the Baoulé, felt shunted aside by Houphouët-Boigny's rapid rise, but he had organized his party on a multi-ethnic basis which did much to defuse their animosity. Relations with metropolitan French politics were more difficult to handle. Houphouët had initially allied his party with the Communists in Paris for tactical reasons, but this produced serious repressions in the early 1950s when the Communist Party was no longer part of the French government. Once Houphouët broke that affiliation and espoused a policy of cooperation with France the reins of government were transfered quite smoothly, with Houphouët-Boigny becoming the first president of an independent Ivory Coast in 1960.

Since independence Houphouët-Boigny has kept the country economically viable by encouraging foreign investment, and has turned its capital, Abidjan, into a modern glass and stainless steel showcase. He has also begun promoting regional growth by creating, among other things, a new harbour in the south-west, a sugar cane plantation and refinery in the north, and a hydro-electric dam in his own central Baoulé region. This development has wrought inevitable changes. Houphouët-Boigny's birth place, where life was until very recently almost identical to that described in this book, today possesses an airstrip which can accomodate jet planes, a conference hall, a gigantic swimming pool, and half a dozen airconditioned hotels which can receive hundreds of tourists or conventioners.

The necessity of earning money as the Baoulé are drawn into the modern economy, which Father Guerry bemoans in his closing lines, is undeniable. What is also remarkable, however, is that outside a few artificially created urban centers the pattern and pace of daily life still remains similar to what it has been in the past. It is in one such Baoulé village, relatively "untouched" by the outside world, that Father Vincent Guerry has spent the better part of the past decade. In *Life with the Baoulé* he shares his observations and interpretations of that existence with us.

Father Guerry's familiarity with Baoulé life is apparent, as is his preference for it over many aspects of western existence. In his first chapter called the Baoulé Universe, for instance, when discussing the Baoulé's thought processes, he obviously favors what he considers to be the Baoulé's ability to intuit or "taste" a fact or event over that of the logical analytical westerner who "sees." There has been considerable controversy in anthropological circles as to whether or not there exists a fundamental difference (in kind rather than degree) between the reasoning process of those living in modern occidental civilizations and non-western peoples. One view, expounded most clearly in the early writings of Lévy-Bruhl, maintains that the "primitive mentality" is characterized by, among other things, a "pre-logical mode of thought" not governed exclusively by laws of western logic. Father Guerry puts himself in this camp (whether consciously or not) when, for example, he explains that a Baoulé who will not be won over by a rational argument can be forced to change his opinion when confronted with the appropriate proverb.

An opposing school of thought, somewhat more prevalent among anthropologists today, holds the belief that the functioning of all human brains is similar, and that methods of thinking do not therefore vary greatly from one society to another. Its proponents from Boas to Lévi-Strauss contend that all people reason in essentially the same way, even if some basic underlying assumptions may differ. The Baoulé's proverb may therefore have just as rational a base as the westerner's argument. The empirical results of cross-cultural psychological experimentation recently conducted among the Kpelle in neighboring Liberia have reinforced the view that observed differences in learning ability between members of different cultures represent differing applications of universal cognative skills, and not different cognative capabilities.

In the chapter on social life Father Guerry describes the outwardly totally communal existence of the Baoulé with its emphasis on group solidarity and lack of privacy in the western sense. He then goes on, however, to point out how this picture belies the extremely solitary, intensely "private" inner life which most Baoulé also live simultaneously. This fundamental fear and loneliness in the midst of such a collective existence is a point that many outside observers had previously missed. It was not until very recently, in fact, that it became the subject of a psychoanalytic study of a related ethnic group in the Ivory Coast.*

Chapter Three, while entitled Marriage, actually covers a much broader area, including matrilineality and female sexuality. African marriage customs, incest taboos and the like have been exploited for their "exotic" value by numerous writers. Guerry instead stresses the importance of the concept of fertility to the Baoulé. He explains that their most powerful "fetish" is the female sex organ, which, as representative of the life force, signifies procreation rather than sexuality. (He also points out in a later chapter that unlike many people for whom the earth becomes the goddess of fertility, the Baoulé's symbolic representation of fertility *is* the female sex organ.) Father Guerry emphasizes how vital children are to the Baoulé, which helps explain the importance and popularity of the Queen Poku story to this day. He also presents the Baoulé woman as liberated in the sense that she is entitled to free unions both before marriage and after, if her husband is away for an extended length of time, provided they result in

---

*Paul Parin et al. *Fürchte deinen Nächsten wie dich selbst: Psychoanalyse und Gesellshaft am Modell der Agni in Westafrika.* (Fear Thy Neighbor as Thyself: Psychoanalysis and Society among the Agni of West Africa), Frankfurt, Suhrkamp Verlag, 1971.

children. It is sterility rather than promiscuity which is considered disgraceful among the Baoulé.

In keeping with the communal nature of Baoulé life, funerals are considered affairs of the entire village. The burial procedures, mourning rites and expressions of condolence which accompany funeral ceremonies and help soften the impact of death are presented in the fourth chapter. Father Guerry also points out several notable exceptions to the communal rule. The news of the death of an important chief is sometimes kept secret for several months for political reasons, and no funerals are permitted for the first three children to die in every family. This seemingly harsh interdiction was initially instituted, Guerry explains, to offset the distress caused by the high rate of infant mortality among the Baoulé.

As with most peoples, the rituals accompanying death are religious in nature as well. Baoulé cosmology is more fully discussed in the following chapter, entitled Religion. The Baoulé are animists, and therefore possess diverse sources of supernatural support. They believe that genii, fetishes, demons and "doubles," sort of alter-egos from the spirit world, affect daily life. The supreme god *Namyia*, on the other hand, has created the world but is not expected to intervene in human affairs. The importance of venerating and propitiating the ancestors is stressed, and the sacrifices to them, masked dances, and oracular pronouncements which still play an important part in Baoulé life are also carefully described here.

In the final chapter, Vincent Guerry attempts to explain why the Baoulé appear happy even in the face of chronic adversity. As in the initial chapter, he contrasts western and Baoulé ways of thinking, here maintaining that the Baoulé have a different conception of time; that they live, essentially, in the present. In so doing the joys of anticipating future happiness may be lost, argues Father Guerry, but so are the difficulties produced by worrying about the future consequences of a present action. An example he uses is that the dread of eventually having to return from a vacation, which spoils many a westerner's holiday, would never occur to a Baoulé. Although this character trait is here seen in a positive light, it has been used in a more pejorative manner elsewhere.

It has been claimed, for instance, that certain impoverished Americans also lack the ability to delay gratification or to plan ahead. In this context not only do these attributes appear less complimentary, but they also tend to carry unfortunate racialist connotations, despite the fact that poor people's difficulties stem from having no money, and not from a different lifestyle. The situation of the Baoulé is different, however, in that they are relatively well off materially compared to many other African groups. And even if most Baoulé villagers do confront "hunger, disease, fear ... [and] death," they have been able to derive strength from the communal institutions and group solidarity described in this book. It is thus interesting that Father Guerry attributes the Baoulé's happiness in spite of these hardships more to a lack of worry about the future than to the vitality of their social organization, given the insight and understanding he reveals in his description of Baoulé institutions.

Paradoxically, as the author points out in his closing lines, these same social and communal institutions are today in jeopardy. They are being corroded by the increasing importance of individual advancement in a monetary economy. The real challenge and dilemma which therefore confronts the Baoulé in the last quarter of the twentieth centry is how to take advantage of what the West has to offer while at the same time preserving the best of the traditional heritage.

The richness and complexity of that heritage is carefully spelled out on these pages by one who has come to know it both as an observer and a participant. In *Life with the Baoulé* Father Vincent Guerry's genuine fondness and admiration for Baoulé culture over that of the West is unmistakable.

Richard Horovitz

A Few Baoulé Proverbs

(With French and English literal translations)

BAOULÉ: Klôklô o dyengbé nu ngben, o kla man tanni.

FRENCH: La navette travaille sans profit, elle n'a pas de pagne sur elle.

ENGLISH: The (weaver's) shuttle works without gain, it needs no clothes.

BAOULÉ: È nyiton, sè è wan nan o yra, o bé man.

FRENCH: Quand tu fais griller, si tu ne veux pas que ça brûle, ça ne cuira pas.

ENGLISH: When you cook and are afraid the food will burn, it will not get done.

BAOULÉ: Baka bo o su sama kungba su, o kpa.

FRENCH: L'arbre qui met tous ses fruits sur une seule branche se déchire.

ENGLISH: The tree that grows all its fruit on one branch will tear apart.

BAOULÉ: Sè è wan nan man éwia bô wo sin, anglô ta man wo kunu.

FRENCH: Si tu n'acceptes pas que le soleil te frappe le dos, la lune ne te caressera pas le ventre.

ENGLISH: If you won't let the sun burn your back, the moon will not soothe your belly.

BAOULÉ: Gua bô tyèlè o ti man liké tolè.

FRENCH: On peut rester longtemps au marché sans rien acheter.

ENGLISH: One can hang around the market for a long time without buying.

BAOULÉ: Atin nuan baka sran kwla o sin, o bô i kanni.
FRENCH: L'arbre situé au bord d'un sentier, reçoit des coups de tous ceux qui passent.
ENGLISH: The tree that grows on the edge of the path receives blows from everyone who goes by.

BAOULÉ: Nantilè o a wié man, bé sa tôtôlè o wié man.
FRENCH: Tant que la marche n'est pas terminée, le balancement des bras n'est pas fini.
ENGLISH: Until you stop walking, your arms continue to swing.

BAOULÉ: Sè è fa waka ngbli è tro sin, o güé man, san è fa kanganfuè gua su.
FRENCH: Si tu n'as que du gros bois pour allumer ton feu il ne prendra pas; il faut y ajouter des brindilles.
ENGLISH: You cannot start a fire with big logs alone; you must add kindling.

BAOULÉ: Klaklô! o lè man ablé ngumi, o lè man manda ngumi.
FRENCH: Beignet! il n'y a plus de maïs seul, il n'y a plus de banane seule.
ENGLISH: Doughnuts! no longer is there cornmeal or bananas alone.

BAOULÉ: Kan doluwa sin, lè yè dyésé o sin.

FRENCH: Là où passe l'aiguille, là aussi passe le coton.

ENGLISH: As goes the needle, so goes the thread.

BAOULÉ: Bé kan man ngua, ngua bô.

FRENCH: On ne joue pas en assistant à un jeu.

ENGLISH: You cannot play by watching others.

BAOULÉ: Sè bé kpu wo dyabué su, nan sé kè: "nan mi wunen bié".

FRENCH: Si tu te blesses à la jambe, ne dis pas: "cela ne fait pas partie de mon corps".

ENGLISH: If you injure your leg, don't pretend that it's not part of your body.

The Baoulé Universe

Thirst for unity, the desire for cohesion, seems to be the deepest aspiration of the Baoulé: to stick as closely as possible to one another, be the other a deity, the universe, or the clan.

Western man finds security in establishing orderly limits in the area both of ideas and of daily life. Clarity of thought is for him a sign of intelligence. Products of graeco-roman heritage, we have acquired our passion for clarity and precision from Greek philosophy and Roman law, subsequently fortified by the influence of Descartes and Locke.

We believe in the scientific method. Ideas must be precise. They must be scrutinized, analyzed, classified. Each idea must be separated from its neighbor by a fence so as to keep its true identity.

Here is an example. Meeting a Baoulé with a little boy, I ask him "Is he your son?" He says yes, he is. But I want to be sure, so I narrow down my question: "Is he your real son? From your own body?" No. So I explain to him that this means he is not his own son. He replies "He is not my bodily son, but he is my real son." At this point, I am lost. He insists that the boy is his real son, even though not physically. To me, "real son" and "adoptive son" are contradictory ideas, separated by a strict boundary of fact. Whereas to the Baoulé they are overlapping, and can both be simultaneously true.

Another example. For a week after he dies, a man's family will put a dish of food in front of his house every evening for him to come home and eat during the night. While I am talking with the family one morning, I point out to them that the departed member did not come back to eat the food, as it has obviously not been touched. They reply "The food is still there, but he has eaten." To my western mind, either the food is intact, so he has not eaten; or there is some missing, which he may have eaten. To them both things are simultaneously true. The food is still there. He has eaten it. They see no contradiction in these two statements.

It seems to me that many misunderstandings between the West and Africa would disappear if, on one hand, Africans would look at things more logically, and on the other, if the West realized that there is not only black and white, but in between there is a whole grey area; that between day and night there is dusk, which is both light and dark, a mixture without clear boundaries.

To feel secure, white man has to have order in his daily life. Things must be arranged and scheduled so that everything will be done at the right time and place.

There is a time for work: eight hours scheduled in office, shop or field. Family life takes place separately, in the home. Social life has its time and place at the club, the swimming pool, the union. Religious life is relegated to certain days, there are certain hours set aside for prayer, in special places serving this sole purpose: churches, synagogues, mosques. Religious life must stay strictly where it belongs, without encroaching on work or fun.

A Westerner feels secure only when he can

define and place his activities. He is not at peace until he has settled his accounts, calculated his annual balance, seen the reports and the statistics. In other words, he has to know exactly where he stands at any given moment.

Furthermore, he has to know where he is in relation to others. "What is my exact place in this society, in this group?" He feels uncomfortable unless his role is precisely defined. Might that not also be the dilemma that bothers the priest in our contemporary western world?

Africans recognize this obsession for precision and organization as a characteristic of white man. For instance, the Baoulé had been planting corn long before the French arrived. They threw the seeds haphazardly between the yams, the gumbo, the tapioca, and it grew. Then white men arrived to tell them to plant the corn in straight rows and regular intervals. Ever since then, corn grown in that way has been called "white man's work." Counting, measuring, separating, straightening . . . white man's specialty.

In contrast, the Baoulé needs union, communion; he likes fluidity, mixture, mystery. He abhors cutting, separating, clarifying, specifying. He fears isolation. He needs to feel surrounded, included, not to feel alone. Solitude is synonymous with evil. The sorcerer is solitary. When one sees a man leaving alone, walking away from the group, away from life, it is obvious that he has evil in mind; he will presumably associate with the devil, the enemy of all life. The desire for union is so strong that it seems that a good part of the Baoulé religion stems from a terror of solitude, a need for this security.

In 1715 the Baoulé migrated in small groups from Ghana. They came with their three great divinities—Heaven, Earth, Ancestors—symbolized by the great tam-tam and the royal thrones. But nevertheless, they were seized by fear. They felt isolated in this forest peopled by enemies—the Gouro—and by dangerous animals; they were but few in number, and their groups were widely dispersed. It was at that point that they felt the need of surrounding themselves by enough divinities to protect them from all sides. Appealing to the many mysterious forces of nature around them, they created a multitude of divinities. They tried in every way to domesticate these invisible, threatening forces, by offering them sacrifices, prayer, and libations. The mysterious powers are innumerable: water, rocks, trees, plants of potent poison; the hunting net, and the numerous objects of personal adornment, sculpted in wood or molded in clay. Not to forget psychological aids: omen, confession, incantation, healing rites, all of them tranquillizers of amazing potency.

Their gods are never far away. You are literally immersed in divinities, you cannot take a step without meeting one. I remember the time when I took a dying woman to the hospital. Before leaving the compound, we had to sacrifice a chicken to the ancestors. Then the relatives accompanying the sick woman in the car started a long litany. Crossing the brook, we had to slow down to invoke these powerful waters; at the top of the hill, the family sent supplications to the large rock that dominates the whole region; then there was the thick bush where the spirits of the earth reside; and the final stop under that great protector, the baobab tree. And I said to myself: "What other religion is there that has gods so close to man?"

Submerged in divinity, the Baoulé is also in union with the physical universe. Man and things are friends, bound together for better or worse. Earth, for example, is a person. She listens to what people are saying, and repeats it to the dead. She suffers with the villagers: when a man dies, she becomes so depressed that she stops producing; a goat will have to be sacrificed to console her. She is also capricious, as women are said to be; if she takes a dislike to rice, for instance, the harvest is doomed, no matter how carefully planted and tended.

On the other hand, man's failing can cause serious disturbances in the universe. Incest will stop the rain from falling and produce prolonged drought. If a certain wood is used to build a fire, the cattle will die. A serious fight in a field may ruin the harvest of its proprietor.

The Baoulé spends all day long with living things. When he starts to cultivate his field and forces his hoe into the ground, he apologizes to the earth: "Pardon me, Earth, for hitting you this way. I do not mean to be unkind, but I need you to feed me and my family. Please help us." When he goes hunting, he speaks to his net and asks it to favor him by helping him catch a lot of game. In crossing a river, he will say "Excuse me, I do have to cross you, please don't kill me." Before eating, he sets aside a little food as an offering for the statuette in the corner of his dwelling. Before drinking, he will spill a few drops of palm wine on the ground so as to invite Heaven and Earth to come and drink with him. And at night, he and his wife face the most powerful of all divinities: Fertility.

Sickness itself is personalized as a messenger to be respected. That holds true even of smallpox, that virulent disease that can wipe out an entire village. It is called "the pretty disease," and the person who succumbs is not pronounced dead but is said, discreetly, to have "returned upon himself." It is most important to speak of smallpox politely so as not to hurt her feelings, in the hope that she may leave without having done too much harm. By the same token, you must never say that you have been bitten by a snake, but rather "a climbing vine surrounded my leg"; the snake hears our words, might take offense and return for revenge. It is therefore better to refer to it as a little vine that delicately enlaces our leg.

The attitude of the Baoulé toward the universe significantly shapes his vocabulary, as it is at the very center of his soul. Rare are abstract words. What we call "joy," he expresses with the feel of freshness: "My heart has fallen into the water." Our concept of generosity evokes in him a color, the color of pure white. He will say "You have chalk in your stomach" to tell you how generous he thinks you are. Sadness is seen as a fog, a mist: "I am covered by warm steam." Anger is expressed as fire. "My heart has put fire in my stomach." Calling for concentration, the Baoulé says "I am taking this object and putting it in the corner of my eye."

Not only his vocabulary reflects this preoccupation with the forces of nature. Every conversation is filled with parables drawn from that universe. Thus, an elder of the village asked his neighbor one evening: "Remember those trees that we planted together? Where is their fruit?" His son who had been to (French) school and was therefore not familiar with allegoric ways of talking, had to ask for explanation of the question. It turned out that his father had lent the neighbor some money that should have brought interest. The forces of nature are thus constantly in evidence in the Baoulé language, by image, symbolism, story, and proverb.

This concrete, pictorial vocabulary does not prevent the expression of general or universal ideas. On the contrary, symbol and image are often better adapted to profound thought than are pure abstractions. The Baoulé, too, have their "wise men." By proverbs and stories—simple as they may seem to the "sophisticated"—they have constructed a philosophy as valid as any.

It is in their fathering of knowledge, their awareness of facts, that the Baoulé adhere most closely to the forces of nature, and differ most from our ideas and methods.

Our first need, as Occidentals, is to *see* clearly when we want to understand a thing or an event. "I see" is the expression we use to mean that we have understood. But to see well, you must not be too close to the object; you have to step back, gain perspective, look at it from a distance. Thus, we separate our children from their environment to give them an education: they go to school. There, in order

35

to make them understand this universe that they have left, we interpret it to them on paper, in books, by maps. And we ourselves, when we want to go into profound thought, we retire to a quiet place, away from noise and from the disturbing sound of life. Do we really try to know ourselves?—When we do, we turn ourselves inside out in introspection, we analyze our thoughts, our feelings, our actions as though we were spectators of a film. Furthermore, we consider it next to impossible to write contemporary history because we are too close to it, we need perspective. Only twenty-five or thirty years from now may we be able to judge "objectively" the events that are happening today.

Not only do we seek perspective in regard to our universe, we have to take it apart to understand it, and analyze the components. We are bothered by things that are mixed together and imprecise. This occidental discomfort starts at an early age. "Why does water flow? Why does fire burn? Why? Why? Why?" asks the western child. We instinctively search out all contributing elements. And adult value judgments are based upon scientific research and proof.

I listened one day to a European agriculture specialist who was explaining to the villagers why rice should be planted in rows, rather than scattered. "First, you waste less time in weeding; second, the water runs off more evenly; third, harvesting is easier ... etc." This is typically Occidental: as soon as all the elements are known, an equitable judgment can be made. And we do not engage in action until we have made a value judgment. A job is first examined from the outside, pro's and con's are weighed, and only then is it undertaken. Action needs motivation; the stronger the motivation, the more effective the action will be.

A Baoulé faced with an object or an event will not want to see it as much as to *taste* it. To understand a thing, he has to internalize it, experience it, "eat it" (*bé di*). The impact is sensual rather than visual. Only physical contact will enable him to understand this thing completely, to find out whether it is "sweet" or "bitter."

In the village, there is never any theoretical instruction of custom. Never, for instance, will a child be called away from his work or play to learn the principles of animism. Rather, and much more effectively, he will learn by living, by "eating" it. He will taste all the sweetness and bitterness in sharing the joy of the dances and sacrificial meals on one hand, and the contagious terror at the arrival of the Great Mask on the other. Animism will thus enter under his skin rather than into his head.

One of the important events in Baoulé life is the judgment, the village meeting. Our occidental procedure progresses on a straight, logical line: facts, witnesses, articles of law, judgment, punishment. Things move according to known regulations. The Baoulé council, however, gives the impression of moving in a circular manner; things do proceed, but slowly and in spirals.

The meeting is set for sundown on the village square. But it will not begin at any specific moment, for it flows with the life of the village, which continues without interruption; everybody eats, washes, and arrives when he is ready; a mother continues to bathe her baby in the middle of the group; two men finish the game of *warré* they had begun, which will not prevent them from listening and even participating.

The subject is not approached directly, so as not to risk hardening the position of the adversaries. Quite different things are discussed, along the lines of what the Romans called "captatio benevolentiae." Though the meeting has been called to deal with a case of adultery, it starts with a conversation about some sheep that have eaten the neighbor's corn. One thing follows another. There are stories, proverbs, events of long ago. Everybody has the right to speak. It takes a long time, the moon has set, and the meeting still goes on. Some people fall asleep, and wake up when called upon. Many hours are thus lived together. The accused and the plaintiffs have very freely expressed their views and feelings. Little by little, in this living spontaneity, the truth has become apparent. Everybody finally knows who is right and who is wrong; they have "tasted" together, and felt where the bitterness and where the sweetness was. The chief did not have to intervene, he was sitting to one side of the group, listening, and at the end he simply put into words what everybody felt, what everybody knew already.

This constant immersion in the universe and the flow of life keeps the Baoulé from introspection. He does not know how to get inside himself, how to analyze his thoughts and emotions, and he therefore cannot explain what he is feeling. The Occidental who has "seen" can easily describe his view of things;

the Baoulé has "felt": how can one describe sensation? Asked why he did something, he will reply, "For no reason." I say to myself, "He is not honest with me, he is hiding his real feelings." But my judgment is wrong, for with the best of intentions he is incapable of telling me what is going on inside him. When I explained this phenomenon to a group of Baoulé, one of them rose and thanked me because, he said, "white men are always telling me that I am not frank with them. I feel something in here" pointing to his belly, "but I don't know how to express it in words."

Analysis is repugnant to the Baoulé. He feels comfortable in the softness and fluidity of mystery, with no desire for the question "why." Even his children, when they pass through the questioning age, will incessantly want to know "where are you going? what are you doing? what do you have in your hand?" but almost never "why?".

In the course of all the research that is now going on in African villages, the Baoulé are baffled by the many "why" questions which they can answer only obliquely. "Why matriarchy?"—"Because our ancestors lived that way." "Why have you no coconut palms?"—"Because the earth does not like them." "Why did that man recover from his illness?"— "Because the day of his death has not yet come." They are afraid of "why" because it corresponds to the great evil feared above all: isolation. The Baoulé believe that this "why" separates, dissects the very elements of life itself; at which point everything would crumble.

I once watched a class on sex education, geared to illiterate Baoulé. Male and female physiology was demonstrated and explained in diagrams and pictures, as was the development of the fetus. It was all very clear, actually too clear, for at the end of the session people were saying: "We saw a lot of things on that screen, but that is not the way one has children; there is something invisible behind all that, something one cannot see, the mystery of fertility and of life. And that is where truth is." To them, what can be clearly seen is not life, is not true.

Nor does truth for them lie in the world of the living that we can watch around us: it is too clear to be true, these are people that one can see and hear, this is a world of pretense and falsehood. The "village of truth" is the world of the ancestors surrounding us, too mysterious a world to fathom: that is where true life is. Where there is no mystery there can be no truth.

Does that mean that the Baoulé is ignorant of the principle of causality? that he cannot trace effect back to cause? No; rather, his intuition encompasses cause and effect simultaneously, without wanting to separate them. This story may serve as an illustration. I had been in the village for a year when a French newspaper man came to do a survey on literacy; for this purpose, he called a meeting of the elders whom he questioned. Seeing me go by in the distance, he asked the men who this white man was. They replied "A priest." "And what is he doing here?"—"We don't know." The journalist insisted: "But after all, he has been here for a whole year, and you still don't know why?" It was explained to him that according to

Baoulé custom it would be a serious breach of courtesy to ask a stranger "what are you doing here?"—"O.K." said the newsman, "but it makes you look pretty stupid to other white men if you don't know why this man is here. . . ." So the next day, the chief called together the elders and asked me to come. "Tell us why you are here, so that we can answer those white men when they come back." So I explained to them that I am here because I enjoy being here, that I like them very much and that, if some day they wanted me to tell them about God, I would gladly do so. They burst out laughing. "Well, we've known that all along!" They knew, or rather they sensed it. A human being present and living among them—why dissect him? By separating his presence and his motivation, a piece of life would escape, and he would come out less alive.

Boileau has said "Whatever is well perceived can be clearly stated, and the words to express it come easily." He is right when it is a matter of reasoning. But for intuition, it is different.

When an elder says to me "don't do that" or "that man is not good" and I ask him why, he cannot answer. My first reaction will be to assume that he is talking without thinking. But I have learned from experience that an African often has quicker and surer judgment because he does not lose himself in the labyrinths of logic. He will not be able to explain the motives of his judgment, but by intuition he will go faster and further. Less inhibited by reflection and introspection, he is open to the world of sensation and emotion, and thus able to perceive shades and details that escape us.

Our decisions are made by a long process of weighing evidence step by step, and requiring proof for everything; only after this is done will we risk leaping into action. The Baoulé dives into action first, and by acting he can "taste" whether it is good. Thus, the formal "engagement" that our young people make before marriage is senseless to him. How can you get to know a girl before you have had several children with her? Only experience can tell.

Because he does not accept the need for motivation, the Baoulé will readily submit to unexplained orders. As soon as he recognizes the power, goodness, or superiority of a person, he is ready to do whatever is asked. If the Commissioner orders the road to be cleaned up, it is done without questioning the purpose: it might be for a celebration, or the arrival of an important visitor, or whatever: nobody asks. The prophet of a new religion can decree interdiction after interdiction, the faithful will follow him blindly: "Just tell us what to do. You are the one who knows, that is all that is needed, it would do us no good to know the reason for these taboos."

So how would one proceed to effect a change of opinion? White man resorts to reason. If somebody is angry, discouraged, obstinate, we "reason" with him, we bring arguments to bear, proofs to try to improve his outlook. This would be useless with a Baoulé. But great effect is achieved with a story or a proverb.

I was walking into a village one day, and was about to enter a compound when someone shouted "Get out of here, white man, I won't have you set foot in my yard." Taken aback, I tried another compound and was received with perfect courtesy; so I told about my misadventure. That family, it seems, had had very bad experiences in the past with white men: pillage, torture, rape; thus their continuing anger. I wondered whether there was a possibility of appeasing this old rancor? The neighbor thought for a moment, then told me to go back and say to the chief: "If the lizard retraces his steps, that won't break his back." No sooner said than done. I simply repeated the proverb, and a complete transformation took place. The old man beamed, asked me to sit down, and we chatted for a long time.

Where does this power of the proverb come from? When we whites are faced with imagery and symbolism, our guards are up, for to us comparison does not spell reason. For a Baoulé, a proverb is a slice of life, a truth that speaks to him, that sends him vibrating with the universe and sways him toward agreement.

Here, I think, is where we come to the bottom of the problem. Whereas the Baoulé is grounded in the universe to the point of being barely distinguishable from it, our civilization has taught us to stand off at a distance, to dispel our irrational fears of powers hidden there, to master the world and use it to our advantage. But by that very fact we have lost our sensitivity toward the world. And that is the abyss that separates us from Africa. One can always adapt to a culture, learn its language, even the mode of thinking. But sensitivity goes by default in such an adaptation. Our deep emotional reflexes were conditioned in our early childhood, and it is not within our power to feel differently. I can go on and on quoting proverbs, I know their potency from witnessing their astounding impact on the souls of the Baoulé, but they have no effect on me. I have learned to tell stories; I can anticipate the burst of laughter from the audience at a certain passage; I laugh with them because they are laughing, but I will never really feel the subtlety of the hidden joke.

> *"The transplanted tree never*
> *gives as beautiful shade as the*
> *one that has grown here."*
> (Baoulé proverb)

Social Life

The tourist who travels in Egypt, Italy or China is immediately struck by the grandeur of these ancient civilizations. The glory of the past is strikingly present. Surrounded by splendid architecture, monuments, paintings, manuscripts, he cannot escape immersion in their spectacular accomplishments.

The Ivory Coast is different. Here are societies based on oral communication, not tangible history. As there are no monuments, no architecture, no written records, the casual visitor may easily deduce that all civilization is lacking and that this is a blank page which must be filled by importing his western culture. That was the reaction of colonial administrator Nebout after his sojourn in Baoulé country; he wrote in the magazine *A Travers le Monde* (Dec. 15, 1900): "The Baoulé are generally not intelligent, and totally lacking in moral quality: they have neither dignity, nor courage, nor energy; they have no special aptitude and are mediocre in everything." Even now, when European tourists see the peasants drinking water from stagnant ponds and mixing cow dung with clay for the floor of their houses, they are apt to exclaim "Those savages!"

This is in fact a different culture, more difficult to understand than those transmitted in books and in stone. It is inscribed in daily life, the subtleties of ancient tradition still throbbing with vitality. Here, in the villages of West Africa, the past is preserved in present customs as can be seen, for instance, in the magnificent architecture of social relations among the Baoulé, the delicate structure of gentle harmony in their daily life. By looking carefully at the depth of feeling manifested in every humble gesture, we may be able to build a bridge of comprehension between our two cultures.

The silent depths of the forest, the constant close contacts with nature, have formed the Baoulé heart. Understated discretion is the special distinction of their polite social behavior. Nothing here compares with the sumptuous feasts in Arabian palaces where one course follows another in a sequence of culinary refinement, planned and presided by a host with the elaborate courtesy of earlier royal centuries.

Here, meals are eaten outdoors, on the ground. There are no individual plates, no eating utensils. The head of the family invites you to dip your hand in the communal dish; you pull off a piece of *foutou*, a starchy dish made of yams, or you take a handful of rice, dip it into a highly spiced sauce, roll it into a manageable lump in your right hand, and eat. Lambs and kids prowl around in search of scraps. There is no polite conversation, no display of wealth. It may be surprising to see no object of art displayed; but on closer inspection, the visitor will notice the intricate design woven into the robes of the chief, the fine carving on his chair, the delicate sculpture on the wooden rice ladle; and he will learn to appreciate the subtlety of the understated remark addressed to him by a member of the family.

This proud people hates servitude, respects the independence of others. An ostentatious display of beauty or excessively courteous manners might deprive the visitor of the opportunity to form his own opinion. The Baoulé do not try to please everybody or be liked by everybody. They are reluctant to disclose the wealth of their inner selves. It takes time and conscious effort to uncover these shyly concealed treasures of heart and mind.

One of the first things that the white explorers noticed about the Baoulé was their extreme cleanliness. Dirt, to them, symbolizes evil and death. The family is up before dawn. After washing themselves, the women take their brooms and sweep house and yard with care. Excrement is carried off to the brush. All household objects are tidily put in their place, mortars and pestles in one corner, gourds hung from hooks on the low ceiling. Though the floor is merely stamped earth, it is spotless; the hearth is as clean as though it had never been used; all garments are neatly folded and stored in a basket. A casual visitor can stroll through the compound during the day and admire all this, for houses and yards remain open while the family is working in the fields. Theft does not exist: the Baoulé consider it mortal sin.

As the sun rises, the woman will leave the village, nibbling an ear of corn for breakfast. Her little daughter trots behind her with a twig in her mouth that she uses as a toothbrush. Vanity knows no age. Her older sisters may have clothes to show off, but she is still naked, so all she has to display are her shiny white teeth, scrubbed with great vigor.

One of the extraordinary things to a person from a western culture is the variety and intricacy of greetings. Our woman, at sunrise, may greet a man by saying, "The day is growing," to which he replies "This is the freshness of the morning." As she walks briskly, she passes a more leisurely villager. "You are the first!" "And you are the last," says he, "what is the latest news?" "I was the last," she encounters, "and look! I have caught up with you." Only after considerable preliminary remarks can the conversation really begin. Meeting a man coming from the opposite direction, she will try to guess from his pace, his manner, or the load he is carrying, whether he comes from the fields or from another village; and her greeting will be chosen accordingly.

Arriving in the field, the wife will join her husband who had started earlier while she was getting the children ready. Greetings will start all over again, for courtesy is just as important within the family. It is charming to hear a little girl who has barely started to speak greet her father at work. "Be of good cheer, dear father." "The air is cool, my daughter; isn't this a beautiful morning?" "Father, the sun has risen. My best wishes for a good day of work." And then the mother will take over with a similar litany.

It is almost impossible for a foreigner to learn the innumerable greetings that vary by person, time of day, and circumstances. I once started to make a list, but gave up after ten pages of close writing. The Baoulé, on the other hand, cannot understand how western people can manage with the uniformity of that short, simple greeting "Bonjour! ça va?" with which they always address him.

At noon, "when the sun stands still above our heads," a fire is made with the fire-brand brought from the village in the morning, and a large yam is roasted to feed the family. Should anybody pass by, he is invited to share the lunch. If he accepts, the head of the family cuts a few branches from the nearest palm tree and weaves them together quickly to make a seat for the guest. The yam is divided, and everyone gets a little less to eat so that the voyager can be fed. Nor will he be allowed to leave with empty hands; he will be given a few yams or peanuts or whatever is being harvested. He, in turn, will reciprocate by clearing a few feet of land, or building a few mounds, or weeding, to show his affectionate feelings for those he is obliged to leave as he goes on his way. And in leaving, he calls back "Hey! we will stay together!" to which they reply "Yes, we shall meet again over there!"

Evening is the time for visiting. The carved door of the compound creaks open. A man enters. With a sweeping gesture of his right arm, he says "Gentlemen, it is getting dark. Ladies, it is getting dark," while his left arm releases his robe to the waist. (One must always greet his own sex first.) "Night is falling," replies the chief of the compound.

A child runs to bring the best stool for the visitor. The father says "sit down and rest." There follows a long silence, so heavy a silence that one would feel embarrassed or even insulted if one did not know the custom. Actually, the idea is to give the visitor time to catch his breath, to regain his composure. The child, in the meantime, has brought a little water in a coconut shell; he bows, and presents it to the visitor with his right hand while supporting his right elbow with his left hand. The chief then rises slowly and goes to shake hands with the visitor. "Night is falling," he says, and this *"nia aossi o!"* is echoed in chorus by the whole family. It would be difficult if not impossible to render in English the long litany of courtesy that follows. It ends when dinner is ready, and the mistress of the house comes toward her guest and says "your thing is here," an oblique way of inviting him to eat. It would be considered miserly to ask anybody whether he wanted anything; that would sound as though it were not freely offered. Rather, one should say "I am bringing you some chicken" or whatever it is.

After dinner, everybody assembles under the big tree in the village, where the host honors his guest with a jug of palm wine. Animated by this strong drink, the Baoulé will become talkative. There seems to be no end to the songs, proverbs, and stories. Even there, however, a certain degree of decency is maintained. "Even when drunk, an egg does not walk on rocky ground" says a proverb.

I remember an occasion at such a party when a cry of indignation arose against a child who had made an indecent noise. The poor little thing ran away to hide, and was not seen for the rest of the day, while one of the elders apologized to me for him. They tell a story as an example of heroism about a child who was sitting next to his father during a public meeting. When the father had the same accident, the boy rose spontaneously and declared that he himself had committed this indecency, thereby saving his father's honor.

It is said that these assemblies become rather bawdy, as can be judged by the raucous laughter. To be specific, it is true that the Baoulé enjoy realistic descriptions in their stories, but there is nothing unhealthy in them for the very reason of their open simplicity that leaves no room for shady implications. They do laugh. In fact, the forest may resound with the echo of roars of laughter of young and old when a new bawdy tale is told about that proverbial spider, Akendewa, and how he outwitted the hyena. But the Baoulé, as all Africans, also know how to smile. Smiles range from barely perceptible expressions of sarcasm to deep emotion, proof once again of great sensitivity.

Where does this joy come from that explodes from all compounds as soon as the moon has risen? You hear nothing but laughter, song and dance to the rhythm of the drum. I believe the deep happiness comes from this solidarity. The solid, firm unity of the village represents for them an indestructible rock of security.

As to the political structure, there is one sole authority, that of the chief surrounded by the elders. He is elected by the village. He can be dismissed if it is found that he is not sufficiently cognizant of customs or proverbs; his power is tempered by that of the soothsayer. This government is more democratic than autocratic, as all large decisions are made in public meetings where everybody, including women and youth, can have a say.

The whole village actually governs itself. Children do not belong to their mothers and fathers but rather are the property of the lineage, of the village which is responsible for them and for their education. The individual is bound to the group; life was given

51

him by the village and it is through the village that he continues to live; should he cast himself off from the village he would be but a dead branch. For a while, he may be able to wander away from this source of life but, as the proverb says, "A dog with a broken leg very quickly finds his way home." At the slightest trouble, any Baoulé will come back to the village.

This unity is felt most strongly during the important moments of life. At birth, the whole village is there. As soon as the cries of a woman in labor are heard, all the women come running to help her, while the men assemble on the village square in as much anguish as if it were their own wife. When finally the birth is announced, all join in a formidable shout of joy. Thereafter, the father calls at every house to thank the villagers, for he feels that it is to them that he owes his child. They then reciprocate by visiting the new mother to thank her for having given them a baby. Thus it is true that the whole village shares in giving birth, giving life.

Illness?—If somebody falls sick, every man and woman will visit him before going to work in the morning; after supper, they will all come again to find out how he is feeling. A sick European or American who feels no need for this solidarity would suffer additional fatigue from this procession; it provides the Baoulé with reassurance and comfort. It would be a great mistake to leave a sick person alone. The group is worth as much as the best medication: it spells life!

Death, of course, is the supreme moment to show village unity. The drums are sounded as soon as somebody dies. Work stops. Everybody returns from the fields to be with the deceased and his family. The funeral is decided by the whole village, and permission for the burial cannot be given until everybody concurs. For this purpose a member of the family has to go from house to house to present his apologies. The deceased, of course, belonged to the whole village. He was in the custody of one family, and significantly the term for his death is "he has broken" (*o asaki*), as though he had been carelessly dropped. "Excuse us for not having taken better care of him, for having let him die," to which the other replies, "I pardon you." It happens, however, that the villagers do not accept the excuses because they feel that the family had neglected their duty to the deceased. It then becomes a matter of increased supplications which finally succeed in obtaining the necessary pardon, and sometimes it is late at night before the corpse can be buried. The funeral ceremonies then last one or two weeks, or even longer.

The international organizations working on economic development are scandalized by this waste. There is statistical evidence of the huge annual number of working days lost, in addition to non-productive expenditures for wine, cloth, etc. Harvest suffers terrible damage during these workless days. There is no question but that the elimination of the funeral rites would substantially increase the material wealth of the village. But has the West not lost some happiness by allowing economic considerations to surpass those of friendship? Living together and sharing those intense days of mourning have a human value that can never figure on the balance sheet of economic inquiry.

Woman Bathing Baby

Man Weaving

57

Woman Cooking Foutou

Woman Spinning

Baoulé Compound

Baoulé Chiefs at Meeting

*Men Dancing

*Baoulé Girls

* Five Boys

And, for that matter, tradition forbids the accumulation of individual wealth. Nobody is allowed to appropriate anything, all necessary goods are communal. The land belongs to everybody, as does the whole village. On, say, a Wednesday morning, the elders will give the word to the villagers, and everybody will go to work, the men cutting stakes, reeds and grass while the women draw water and work up the earth. By night, the homeless man has his house. All he needs to do is to treat the workers to a little palm wine to thank them. In return, everybody can enter the home when he chooses; people can come in just to sit down, or to spend the night; they can help themselves to what minor objects they need, such as fire, water, tobacco, tools. Everybody is at home everywhere.

So communal is everything that there seems to be no personal life. Nothing is hidden. Anybody can enter your house and look at everything. If you are discussing a family problem or a marital difficulty and somebody comes in, you greet them and then continue the same discussion. It would be considered impolite if you stopped, or changed the subject. Private conversations are rare and brief; subjects for a confidential talk would usually be the preparation of a supplication or the choice of a gift. Everything is everybody's business. Coming and going, you are pestered with questions: "Where are you going? What did you buy? How much did it cost?" and your basket is opened, your purchases are admired, the peanuts are sampled, the yardgoods unfolded and examined. It would be rude not to ask questions; it is nice to show interest and sympathy.

The hardest thing for a European or American to take when staying in an African village is the total lack of privacy, and the impossibility of having one moment of intimacy with another person. We too are social beings, but our group relations are well defined and limited, always allowing for the importance of time to ourselves: to be alone, away from the crowd, by oneself and with oneself, breathing deeply away from "the other." The Baoulé, in contrast, lives always with the others; it would be quite inconceivable to him to be cut off from the group, even for a few minutes.

Even sleep is a matter of public life in the village. We have been taught to sleep alone, from infancy on; babies are placed in quiet rooms, away from any noise. The Baoulé baby is tied closely to his mother's back, and sleeps when he is tired, regardless of what she may be doing. She will bend over while weeding or scrubbing, she will go dancing at night, she will work in the hot sun—the baby will sleep through everything. I once watched some children at play in the village square. A four-year-old was asleep in the sand; his little brother, age two, was sitting on the older one's head, rocking to the rhythm of his dancing friends. Despite the sweat that dripped from their two bodies, the sleeping child did not wake up until the end of the game when the noise ceased, and life stopped.

A man will take a nap at the entrance of his house; a passing friend will waken him to greet him. He responds to the greeting, then immediately resumes his dreams where they had been interrupted. The older men are still baffled by the weird manners of those first Europeans who came to Bouaké. "If we happened to pass their houses at the time they were sleeping, we were told to take off our shoes and to whisper so as not to waken the White Man!" It seems incredible to them that human presence or sound would disturb a person's sleep.

At first sight, all life seems a shared, communal experience of work, pleasure, pain, flowing like a brook through the village; a group of people assembled, resembling each other like drops of water, devoid of personality, of distinct character. The flow of life would seem to be that of the group, not the individual. But this appearance is deceptive. The Baoulé has a deep personal life that he confides to no one.

The Occidental is well equipped to protect and develop his private life. There is such respect for individualism in our societies that everyone can disclose his deep feelings, can confide in a friend, without the risk of losing his identity. The Baoulé however has to be quite intransigent about his inner life unless he wants it to become completely public. Exterior goods are so firmly owned by all, the notion of public property is so strong, that he feels the need to preserve his inner world entirely for himself, to build an impenetrable wall around it. According to a proverb, "our inner life is like a forest; nobody knows what goes on inside." Words, smiles, embraces are exchanged all day long, everybody is together, nobody is ever alone. But their souls are sealed.

I remember two inseparable friends who spent all their time together, who worked, played, ate together and shared everything. One day, one of them

took the bus to the capital city without telling the
other. Now why would he have informed me who
mean nothing to him? Precisely, I believe, because I
am a stranger; as I am not close to him, my
knowledge would present less threat to his privacy.

We are offended by this lack of candor, and are
tempted to accuse them of insincerity. "They don't
tell the truth." Actually, where we go off the track is
that we are not on the same wave length. If we
wanted to establish full communication, we would
have to share the same intuition and sensitivity. How
can one tell, for instance, whether a given word or
statement is meant to be taken seriously? The Baoulé
guesses; he feels instinctively what is at the root of
the matter, and what is merely thin air.

For us, the word must be the true transmission
of the thought, or else it is a lie. The Baoulé too has
words of truth, for he believes in the power of words
even more than we do: a certain malediction, upon
pronouncement, is as effective as the strongest
poison. But in ordinary life, there are lots of words
that are said merely to keep up good relations, much
as we flash smiles to people around without attaching
much importance to them.

A typical example could be my question "Can
you come tomorrow morning to lend me a hand with
my field?" The man wants to please me; he knows I
will be disappointed if he says no. He therefore
promises to be in my field at daybreak, and I leave
happily. After waiting in vain for my helper next
morning, I am apt to declare "you just can never rely
on these people." But had I been an African, I would
have accepted the man's promise the way it was

meant. I would have understood that he merely wanted to say something nice, and I would have left, saying to myself, "who knows, he just might come to help me tomorrow."

The same thing is true of one of the most frequent and disturbing misunderstandings, when a Baoulé asks you for something. In most cases he is merely trying to say some nice words to you, while we are revolted at what we call "their mendicity": they are always asking for presents. It is important to realize that they do the same thing to each other in the village all the time. So maybe we should try to understand this behavior.

In the West, we take a certain pride in not depending on others, and we admire the dignity of the poor man who prefers to live in misery rather than debase himself by begging. To ask for charity is very humiliating, and one would think twice before making a request, as its refusal would be a devastating disappointment.

The Baoulé prefers to give than to receive, for giving means dominating: a phrase of thanks is "you are mighty." When you give, therefore, you take a chance of humiliating. To avoid the shame of receiving, the Baoulé have designed a complex ritual in which giver and receiver communicate only through the help of a mediator. Soon after my arrival in the village, I intended to present the chief with a certain metal chair that I knew he wanted. Typical white man that I am, I directed my steps toward his compound, chair in hand. But suddenly I was intercepted by one of the village elders who came running across the square and grabbed the chair.

"You go to the fields," said he, "and let us handle this matter." I was quite taken aback, but I obeyed. And not until that evening did I learn what had happened. At the hour when the cheering sound of mortar and pestle calls late workers from the fields, I was met by three elders who explained to me that they themselves had gone to present the chair to the chief, in my name; and they were now thanking me, in the name of the chief. Thus, the chief was not humiliated by the gift, and was not put in the position of having to bow to me and to say "you are mighty."

It is worse never to ask for anything than not to give anything. In fact, it is as bad as not to talk to somebody. A Baoulé will ask for something as easily as he will say good morning or good evening, without really caring very much for the thing he requests. It is quite customary, for instance, when one sees some-one leaving for the market or the city, to say to him "bring me a nice present from there, won't you?" It is obvious that the traveller cannot satisfy everybody but—who knows?—he just might bring something anyway. There's no harm in asking, and it is another way of expressing the wish to remain united: the farewell expression in Baoulé is *é tè o nou*—we stay together.

When I first came to the village, I coldly refused these requests, thereby hurting the feelings of both children and grown-ups who considered my attitude almost insulting. In due course, I got to understand the meaning of these requests; from then on, I promised to buy everything I was asked, and had the pleasure of watching those broad smiles of happiness.

So I return empty-handed. But nobody asks me for the promised scarf, or bread, or candy; nobody is disappointed, as I was not really expected to come back laden with presents. The requests were made primarily to confirm our ties of friendship, to strengthen the expression of desire for my speedy return.

The real meaning of requests is the acceptance of being united, tied together by self-made bonds. The very unity of the village has been woven in the course of time by these exchanges of gifts and services: people tied to one another as closely as the woven threads of cloth. Before markets were introduced, a man with a large crop of yams would give the surplus to his neighbors, and another who had the good luck to kill a buffalo or an elephant would share it with the whole village. The spirit of this sharing is still alive today, though the scale is much smaller. A woman returns from her field with a basket of bananas on her head; a cute child along the path begs her for one, which she gives him with a smile; as she passes the pond, her friends who are washing clothes clamor for their share. There may conceivably not be a single fruit left by the time she gets home. But it does not really matter. She can stroll happily through the compound, asking for some okra here, some peppers there, and soon have all she needs to cook her sauce for dinner.

This sharing, borrowing, exchanging creates a current of empathy, a vital flux that circulates throughout the village. But it is fragile, and can be broken by one single refusal. A person, for instance, who demands reimbursement for damages would be said to have constructed a dam, a dike that cuts the free flow of current. I floundered for a long time in the maze of these intricate customs, and I remember particularly one blunder that I committed shortly after my arrival. I had borrowed a glass; one day it slipped through my hand and broke. True to western custom, I went to the city to replace it. At the sight of this new glass, the man's face darkens with obvious displeasure and he refuses it: I had severed the free-flowing, gracious current, and set up a barrier between us. It took the intervention of one of the elders on my behalf to reestablish communication.

The ties created by this system are very solid. A white man who has received a gift needs to express his thanks only once. Then he is free. The Baoulé remains attached to his benefactor. He must repeat incessantly, "thank you for yesterday! thank you for the day-before-yesterday! thank you for last year!" One of the main attributes of a Baoulé gentleman is gratitude. "He knows what is good; he appreciates beauty." For the Baoulé as for the Greeks, beauty equals goodness. And the height of perfection is to safeguard the bonds that tie us to one another.

Marriage

Childhood

As soon as a baby leaves his mother's back and starts to walk, the boy will follow his father, while the girl lives with her mother. She imitates her in every way she can. As her mother has in the meantime given birth to a baby brother whom she carries on her back, the little girl has to have her own baby; she is given an appropriately shaped gourd that she will lovingly carry around; but it will not be long before she will allowed to strap her real baby brother to her back, though he seems almost as big as she is. When her mother pounds the yams in the mortar, she will try to do the same with some leaves that she has gathered.

Who will initiate her into the mysteries of life? Never will her mother say a word to her about sex or marriage, and the little girl will never ask her any questions: that would be embarrassing. Parents have their separate room, and as soon as the baby is old enough to observe anything, he is housed with his brothers and sisters. Nevertheless, a little girl of four or five knows quite a lot. Information is furnished by the older children, passed down by hierarchy from age to age. A big girl will tell the next one in age what she has just found out, and the information will spread down the line. Further sources of information are matrimonial law suits that are settled in the presence of everybody, even the youngest, and in which often no detail is spared.

The main place where a little girl learns her job as wife and mother is at the water's edge where the women congregate. At dawn, when her brothers follow the men to the fields, she will trot beside her mother to the pond to fetch water and join the gossiping women. She will hear them discuss their female prowess, their domestic troubles, and how they spent the night. The little girl will take it all in. That was the way her mother learned the facts of life, and her mother's mother before her. And if she stumbles on the way back to the village and spills most of the water that she is carrying on her head, she is still proud of the few drops left in the tiny gourd: for she is one of the women.

In the evening, she will sit by her grandmother and listen to endless stories laced with song, mostly about the adventues of Mr. Akendewa with his wife Mrs. Akolou (spiders both, and beloved throughout Africa). These rather ribald stories will initiate the little girl slowly into the psychology, vocabulary, and interdictions of marriage.

Now the moon has risen, and the girls start to dance. These dances are for girls only, though often young mothers with babies on their backs will join them. They are what we would call rhythmic games of considerable variety, clapping of hands in different formation and sequence, falling into each others's arms, throwing one girl into the air. The complex rhythm is maintained throughout the movement by feet, hips, and hands. That rhythm has, practically speaking, entered the very body of the little Baoulé from infancy, when carried on the back of her dancing mother. The songs that go with these dances are full of erotic poetry. All the mysteries of fertility are invoked in thinly veiled symbolism.

During that time, the boys form a circle round the dancers, with mixed emotions of admiration, jealousy, and envy, shouting compliments and insults at them. How clumsy they seem beside these girls who dance so well! They feel humiliated but, at the same time, so fascinated that they cannot tear themselves away to play their own games.

But the following evening they will have their revenge. One of them will disguise himself as *Klô*, the magical spirit (fetish) of little boys. He and his gang will dance through the village at the time that yams are being cooked, and will be given a sizeable lot of boiled yams which they will go and eat alone. The girls, who had been following them with rhythmic clapping, will get none. "Women cannot share the fetish of men" the boys announce solemnly.

Initiation Rites

The rites vary somewhat with the tribes. There are three or four Baoulé tribes that practice circumcision of girls. Others "wash them according to the *atomvlè* rites." Early in the morning, the girl is washed, perfumed, and adorned with beautiful clothes and jewels before presenting herself to the village. She then has to wait for seven days before spending the first night with her betrothed.

In the region where I live (*faafoué, aari*), initiation takes place at the first menstrual period. Never will a girl announce that she had her period:

that would be shameful, and cause people to say she seemed in a hurry to get a husband. But her mother watches, and when she suspects something, she sends one or more of the girl's friends to spy on her while she is bathing. If a girl does not menstruate at the customary age, her parents worry about her fertility, and vaginal lotions made of certain herbs are used to bring on puberty.

As soon as the parents have been notified of their daughter's period, they consult the soothsayer to find out whether the *Blolo Niain* agrees to the initiation. She is the woman who inhabits the abode of the dead, and who had already given birth to this girl before she was born a second time on this earth. This woman, consulted through oracles, consents or sometimes refuses; in the latter case, she may require the *atomvlè* rite, or simply ask for a necklace.

If a favorable reply comes from the abode of the dead, a day is set, and the girl is wakened at cock's crow by old women who hit her with a white cache-sexe. They say: "We are giving you this cache-sexe; you are grown-up now; if you have a child, it will be a child of this house."

The girl begins to cry. Sometimes she will run away and hide in a neighboring village. It may even happen that the girl gets suspicious and escapes when she hears the old women enter who, in that case, throw the cache-sexe after her. Such conduct meets with approval. "She is a good girl, she is chaste; she has escaped." And she will have many suitors. But if she seems happy and "shows no shame," she will be spanked to bring about better feelings.

This white cache-sexe will never be worn. It is

thrown by the roadside as an offering. In earlier days, however, this was the first garment for the initiated. Up to the time of the ceremony, a girl was allowed to wear only a very narrow cache-sexe. Old people remember the happy days when girls were seen completely naked at the weekly market and neverthe-less, they say, there was less irregularity than now when some of them even cover their breasts. Men knew that they could not touch a "naked" girl; they might quietly admire and select, but they controlled themselves. The arrival of white man has spoiled all that.

From the day of initiation on, a girl must have vaginal ablutions every morning before taking any nourishment or cooking for others. She is thought to be "unclean" when she rises in the morning, and not only during menstruation.

But the great change for the initiated is that it has been made known everywhere that the man who loves her may invite her to his house at night. From now on she is at the disposal of her suitors, not for regular marriage—it is too early for that—but to have children: that is what matters most. She could probably have had intercourse with a boy she liked before this ceremony—there are no sexual prohibi-tions in this region—but she would have feared pregnancy while "not dressed": such a child has no right to life. The chief purpose of initiation is to legitimize the child.

Free Union

An initiated girl can respond every night to the call of the man who desires her. There are however some timid girls who keep on refusing because they are afraid of boys. They will have to conform to custom fairly soon though, because their reputation is at stake. Rumors start readily about being "abnormal," not capable of marriage, and her parents will do all they can to get her pregnant as soon as possible: the honor of the whole lineage is at stake. No other way of life is conceivable in the village. There is no word in the Baoulé language for "bachelor" and "virginity"; it would take complicated paraphrasing to explain that a mature girl was a virgin.

A girl may remain faithful to the first boy who called her. She may also try several boys before settling on one. In any case, there has to be a long period of free union before talking about marriage. A girl is available, but she is always free to refuse propositions, and she does so. She cares, of course, about physical beauty, because she wants beautiful children. She also has to be careful to guard against the ever-present danger of incest. According to Baoulé concept, two brothers cannot go after the same girl, and two sisters cannot go with the same boy, even after an intervals of years.

In former days a girl was expected to settle her choice quickly, so that one would know who fathered the baby. But these days, girls are in no hurry to get married. Some even decide to remain free all their lives; among these are the prostitutes, who will have several men in the same night, which the Baoulé consider highly disgraceful.

It is extraordinary that within these very free relations between men and women there still remains an unbreachable chasm separating the sexes—call it modesty, or shame. Men and women are mercilessly teased for any show of affection between them. Never do they exchange confidences or tender words (I am not speaking of people who have seen movies or read novels). People do not kiss or caress; if a man is seen chatting with a woman, he is derisively called a "lady's man," and the same disgrace goes for a woman. This "shame" is even further accentuated after marriage, when it extends to the whole family of in-laws. When travelling, a man will walk at a distance from his wife; when visiting in another village, he hides in a secret corner when eating with her, as it is considered a disgrace to share a dish with a woman not of his lineage.

This shame of showing his feelings makes the Baoulé hide them behind rough behavior. They throw insults at the person they love—not the sort of insults that would lead to fights, but real insults nevertheless, and even blows. The beloved is hit with a switch, hard enough to hurt, or his/her arm is grabbed and twisted. The victim cries out with joy, and is happy and proud of being loved. These manifestations can be rough enough to cause accidents. I have heard of broken arms, and I myself once came upon a very dejected looking girl near the first-aid station. Upon my inquiry, she explained "I was playing with my boy-friend last night on the village square, and I hit him with a stick, but I hit too hard and split his lips, so they are now putting in some stitches."

The only prohibition in these games is to suck your lover's arm until the blood rises to the skin. This sign of great love, practiced by other African tribes, is forbidden to the Baoulé, for they believe that if one of the partners thus "united" should die, the other would follow immediately to the land of the dead, so great is their love.

The Wife and Her Fetish

Man and woman are adversaries who love each other. While mutually attracted, they have to be on guard against each other, armed with their fetishes, so as to maintain an equilibrium of strength. The power of that of the woman is so strong that the man would quickly lose his independence, had he not his own fetishes to protect him.

In addition to matriarchy—of which more later—the wife has the greatest, most powerful fetish in the whole Baoulé culture: her female sex. The serious impact of this magic becomes obvious at the puberty dances of the girls: the solemn devotion in the faces of the spectators while chanting praise of Fertility. So terrible is the power of this fetish that a man is punished by death for seeing it: if he catches sight of a woman during her vaginal ablutions, he must die.

This is the fetish to which one resorts against the worst things: war, epidemics, witch-craft. It is stronger than all the other fetishes combined, stronger even than the Demon. When war breaks out, the men appeal for help to their wives who, clad in white, will dance *adyanou* all day long to forestall the slaughter of their sons and the defeat of their husbands. During a small-pox epidemic they dance *adyanou* all night, completely naked, while the men lock themselves into their houses. If any man had the audacity to cast an eye upon this great fetish, he would die. Even when a sorcerer casts a spell on the village, the goddess Fertility is the one to whom one appeals for help. Then all the women undress at night and dance naked to muzzle the Demon.

As soon as she is initiated, every woman carries this fetish in her own body. A wife who has been humiliated or beaten can turn to her fetish; patting her lower belly with her hand, she points to the culprit who is thereby doomed, sooner or later, to death. The only way he can avoid this punishment is to hurry back with a chicken to appease the fetish. The woman, surrounded by her friends, will then undress and let the blood of the bird run between her thighs to save the culprit from death. They then eat the cooked chicken. No man may participate in this sacrifice.

All initiated women are joined together in an association for the cult of their goddess which only they can perform. The altar is a large clay pot standing upside down on the ground. The priestess is elected for life. After the procession through the village she sits, naked, on this urn, slits the throat of the sacrificial animal, and lets the blood flow around her.

The Wife and Her Husband

In view of this great female power, the male has to mobilize all his fetishes to maintain his independence. Unlike that of the woman, his sex organ is not a fetish; but each man has his own magic attributes that must be respected by his wife.

There are all sorts of prohibitions that a wife must observe so as not to arouse the anger of the male genii. She must never disparage her husband's virility. She must not draw the curtain of the bedroom before her husband comes in at night. A woman always has the right to refuse to spend the night with her husband, but once she is in his room, she cannot turn her back to him or refuse him. A sacrifice is required to make amends for any such transgression.

There are a great many prescriptions to maintain the equilibrium between wife and husband, mostly designed to prevent the wife from feeling superior to him. A menstruating woman is considered impure; her husband must avoid contact with her during this time, even as to entering the room that she is in. During her menses the woman cooks her food separately, even over a separate fire. On certain, prescribed days, women are denied access to the sources of water, wells or brooks; they have to pound their rice and chop their wood outside of the village; they are not allowed to enter the village carrying a cluster of palm seeds or a faggot of fire wood; they must not pound their mortar in the presence of their husband. There is no end to the prohibitions that women must observe; they vary in every village, sometimes even from compound to compound. The majority of taboos are clearly aimed at women.

Nevertheless, the Baoulé woman maintains a certain independence. True, she has accepted the name of wife from the day that the groom's parents came to accept her; but that does not mean that the marriage is really concluded. She expects to be wooed for quite a while thereafter. Her husband will have to come every night to sleep at her house. She may have given birth to three or four children before her parents will let her move to her husband's compound. At this point, she receives the symbolic dowry: what used to be a little gold dust or a five-franc piece has now become four or five thousand CFA (about $20). Her husband also presents her with a bark mat which she must give to her mother: "When I was a baby, I wetted your mat and spoiled it; please take this one to replace it." Finally she moves to her husband's house, and is considered truly married after she has cooked her first meal on the hearth of his compound.

If the spouses start quarrelling, even to the point of physical blows, they are allowed to fight it out; that makes for greater love, it is said. But the following day she will run away from home to test out his true affection. He will then come with bowed head to beg her forgiveness and ask her to come back.

Divorce used to be rare. Now they say, "In the olden days, only the grave would separate a married couple; now, it is a matter of twelve days." Actually, if a couple agrees to separation, both partners take their personal belongings and go home to their respective families without any further formalities. Only if one party refuses to divorce or claims damages does the matter come before the elders.

The Future Mother

If a girl is willing to become a wife, it is because of her great desire to be a mother; a husband, on the other hand, would find it difficult to accept a sterile wife. The infant to be born is the only bond between husband and wife, for it is their only joint possession.

A barren woman lives on the edge of society and, what is worse, she brings malediction to her family, as the matrilineal succession is carried by the girls. No matter how many children the boys may have, the lineage ceases if their sisters are barren. This anxiety stimulates every girl's wish to prove as soon as possible that she can bear children, and her family is proud to know of her pregnancy.

Nevertheless, no matter how happy she is, the girl will never announce this good news to her parents: this is somehow an embarrassing thing of which one must not speak. She will therefore be under close observation, and certain early signs are said to indicate pregnancy: swelling of veins in her breasts, darkening of the nipples; her navel may protrude slightly after eating, her skin may become lighter in color, she sleeps more and, above all, a pregnant woman has a body odor that is unmistakable to the fine nose of the Baoulé: "She has the smell of blood."

Her parents will then ask who the father is. If the girl loves him, she will divulge the name of her lover, and her father will go to his parents with the happy news. If she does not care for him, she may simply say "I slept in the village"; that suffices. Her father will then happily adopt the baby, who will bear his name. The same happens if the alleged father refuses to acknowledge the child as his.

Toward the third month the girl's father or husband will go to consult the oracle to find out whether all goes well. He will procure a goodly quantity of palm wine, and invite all the men of the village to drink with him while waiting for the verdict. There are some sooth-sayers who can even foretell whether the baby will be a boy or a girl, but nobody can cause its sex to change. Only Great Heaven causes fertility, and decides what children are to be born. For a first-born, these consultations must be repeated three or four times during the months of pregnancy, and sacrifices are usually imposed to gain the favor of the many spirits seething around this great event.

A pregnant woman is not excused from any work. On the contrary, the harder she can work and the braver she is, the stronger the child will be. A woman who gives in to fatigue and who takes a nap after meals will have a lazy baby. She must watch out carefully to observe the many prohibitions during this time. She must not eat eggs, or else at the moment of birth "she will be wandering around like a chicken in search of a place to lay her egg." She must not eat rabbit; she must not look at the corpse of a dog, nor particularly at the dangerous *nzomou*, the black fish that attacks babies in the womb. She must make no preparations for her future baby, no beads, no mat, no bracelet, or else she will be sure to miscarry.

There is no prohibition against intercourse during pregnancy, it is even recommended from time to time so as to "feed the belly." Much as the Baoulé insist that the man is the most important factor in conception, they do realize that the woman can do without him thereafter. The father could be far away or even dead, and still all could go well if the woman would "feed her belly" herself, by occasionally drinking water that was poured into the mortar after the yams had been pounded.

Miscarriages are apt to occur only as a result of illness. But before the third month they are not considered miscarriages. It is merely said that "her blood flowed"; for during the first two months, a baby is not yet formed, but is "merely blood." After three months, the baby is said to "settle in the belly," and toward the fifth month he "rises and kicks inside his mother." The fetus has his double (*wawé*) from the third month on. The biological knowledge that the Baoulé has about the evolution of the fetus brings on another prohibition. As one must never bury two corpses in the same grave, the corpse of a pregnant woman must be opened and the fetus removed and buried separately.

A prolonged sequence of miscarriages can so discourage a woman that she may wish to become sterile. For this, it suffices for her son to shout from inside the house, while she is bathing, "Mother, don't have any more children." This malediction always works.

Giving Birth

Occasionally, the arrival of a baby takes the mother by surprise: she thought she had counted the months but seems to have missed one, and the baby is born on the path while she was going to the field to work. It will then be named "*Atoungblé*." Or she may be returning from the river, carrying a bucket of water on her head, when she feels the baby slipping, and will have just enough time to get home to receive the little one in her hands.

But most women do have labor pains, and go the bath-house with many female helpers. Any woman who has given birth knows enough to be a mid-wife, and even some of the very young ones are very competent due to grandmother's prescriptions. First the woman is given an enema to still the pain; then she is seated on the ground. The new-born, however, will not touch the earth, for the women will receive him in their hands.

Men, children, and women who have not given birth are barred from the bath-house. In case of complications, however, help is sought from the men. If the birth is delayed, the father rushes to the sooth-sayer to consult the oracles: somebody in the family must have roused the anger of the spirits, or perhaps the woman was adulterous. It will take a public confession, a sacrifice, and medications to remedy this: a slice of pineapple crushed with the leaves of a certain plant and a hot pepper cut in two (one half must be discarded) are mixed with kaolin and administered in potions and lotions, then massaged into the mother's pubic hair.

As soon as the new-born has emerged, the umbilical cord is tied with palm thread and severed with a knife. Then the women rush outside crying "yee-yee! the woman is saved!" to which the men respond with a resounding "wo-wo." The baby however must not be washed until the placenta is out, which means that a baby may be crying all day and nobody can help it. If the placenta takes too long, the husband is asked to fetch his Baoulé-pants; the women use them for a brisk rubbing of the patient's belly to speed up the placenta. This placenta is then taken by one of the barren women of the village, and buried under the bath-house; she urinates upon it, and then sits for a few minutes on this privileged piece of earth so that she may possibly become fertile.

Now the baby is washed with warm water and soap, and its mouth and tongue are rubbed with lemon. Finally mother and child are taken home, where a charcoal fire warms the mother's body for several days.

Mother and Child

For the next two weeks, the mother cannot leave the compound or show her breasts; the baby must not see the sun. At the end of this period, an old woman comes to get the child to introduce it to light. She lays the baby on the ground below the gutter and throws water upon the thatched roof so that it will splash down on the baby. The baby starts to cry. The old woman picks it up and bathes its head three times with a mixture of palm wine and herbs, while chanting "Here you are with us now; you shall not kill your father or your mother." If there is a sterile woman in the village, she swallows the wine and the herbs to bring her fertility. Finally the baby is exposed to the sun, coated with a second concoction: "You shall conquer the sun."

Even though every mother wants many children, she will avoid spacing them too closely, as the last-born would suffer if replaced too quickly by a new baby. Without any rules or prohibitions, the husband stays away from his wife for six to eight months after birth. It is also advisable for him to wait for the return of her menstrual period, because a baby conceived before that time could be refused by the village.

The child really is the glory of a wife. Her husband's esteem of her will rise with the number of her children. Pre-marital or adulterous children do not mar the happiness of the home, on the contrary: a husband is glad to adopt the children of an unwed mother as his own. And if, during a husband's long absence, his wife has had another child by a lover, it will be immediately adopted by the returned husband. He will, however, try to find out who the culprit was, in order to collect the fine imposed upon adultery; even if he fails, he will happily accept this "windfall"; for his wife, he says, "has gathered another child, and put it aside for my return." He will never give up this child; he considers it his own, and loves it as he would his own flesh, whereas the real father speaks of it as "the child of theft." Such is the value of children to the Baoulé.

Children, as noted, are the only treasure owned jointly by husband and wife, but in matrilineal society they are more attached to their mother than to their father. In case of divorce, children go with the father, but their emotional attachment to the mother never ceases, and it is she who will later be the beneficiary of their largest gifts. This is a natural consequence of the matrilineal system, where it is the mother and her brothers who pass on the wealth. A boy will be cherished and spoiled by his mother's family. When his maternal uncle dies, he and his mother will be the heirs. His father's death, however, will leave him empty-handed. From an early age on, he senses that he is more important to his mother's family than to his father's.

It is true that husband and wife cohabit for the purpose of having children, their only common possession, both emotionally and financially. They know, however, that the fruits of their labor and these very children may disperse in one direction or another. It is here that the wider family ties become important, the man's attachment to his mother, his sisters, his nephews: it is for them that he is working, for they will be his heirs. And his wife, for the same reason, will never break the ties with her mother, her brothers, her nephews.

Polygamy

Why polygamy?—There are those who say the reason is laziness and lust of gain, as women are the best workers and beasts of burden, leaving the man free. This is not correct. Women do work hard. They weed, they grow the vegetables, pound the grain and the yams, cook the food, wash the children, and then sit down to spin the cotton. But unless a polygamous man had inherited enough wealth to afford hired hands, he would have to work overtime to prepare the fields with machete and hoe for his wives. No woman ever clears the land or builds the mounds.

98

Such a man could hope for profit only much later, when his sons are old enough to do the heavy work.

A better reason might be the Baoulé's highly developed artistic sense, and love of beauty. Many are the proverbs alluding to the charms of woman. "If you choose a wife in haste, you will soon see that even your mother-in-law is prettier than she." So, as soon as one wife starts aging, the husband is apt to meet a prettier one whom he prefers.

But the best explanation would seem to be the husband's search for perfection. The way one villager explained it to me was: "Before the cow came to the village, the sheep thought she was very big," and so, when you have only one wife, she tends to become conceited and believe you cannot live without her. She will become more humble after the arrival of a second wife; jealousy, and the fear that you might leave her, will prompt greater effort in trying to please her husband. But soon the next problem arises: the two women are forever quarrelling; to help them get along and strike a balance, you will need a third one. . . .

Nor is a husband ever satisfied with his wives: one has a bad temper, the other is barren, the third is incompetent. So he will continue to search until he has found his dream, the *aounimba klaman*, "the beautiful heart." When he has found her—and she may be the tenth—he calls her *bla ndré*, the princess, for she combines all the best qualities of wife, mother, and hostess. This last is the most important. She is the one who follows all the rules of hospitality. She receives visitors politely and sensitively, her sauces are renowned for their fine flavor, she is the pride of his house. And she is the one whom he will entrust with his money when he is away.

A wife in polygamy is not a slave. She keeps all her rights. When a husband wishes to add a new wife, he must gather his women together, beg their forgiveness at not being satisfied with them, and give his reasons for wanting a new one. "In the midst of water, I am still thirsty!" He then awaits their verdict; he could ignore it only at the risk of seeing them leave, one after the other. When their answer is inconclusive, he appeases them with gifts of clothes and jewels. If even that does not suffice, he summons one of the old women of the village to convince those who are still recalcitrant.

Often the wives welcome a new companion in the home: more of them to work in the fields, to care for the children—who call all their father's wives "Mother," without distinction—and chiefly, more women to amuse them around the fire at night, when the harmattan blows, with stories of the adventures of their youth. It even happens sometimes that a wife will beg her husband to find a new companion, as evenings alone are boring.

However, life is not always serene. Quarrels among the wives are frequent, chiefly from jealousy. A husband must be very careful not to favor one wife before the others. The number of nights he spends with each one is fixed with precision, and no wife would dare to enjoy any special privilege, as all the others would band against her and make her life miserable. When there is serious trouble in the group, however, the husband does not intervene directly, but calls in one of the elders who will investigate and pronounce his verdict, consisting of apologies to be made, and gifts to be presented.

Adultery

According to traditional law, only the wife can be accused of adultery, as the husband always has the right to seek another woman. A husband who suspects infidelity will investigate carefully. When he has found the culprit, he will send his own parents to the parents of the other man with the words "You have walked on my mat." The two families will then appear before the tribunal of the elders. If the man is pronounced guilty, he has to comply with all the demands of the wronged husband who may ask for an ox or a large sum of money, not for himself, but as a sacrifice to the spirits and the ancestors. "Becalm yourselves," he will pray, "and do not harm my wife or her accomplice." Occasionally, the husband will yield to the sincere apologies of the culprit. In that case, he will fetch some palm wine, sit upon the lap of the man who has pardoned him, and take the first sip. The plaintiff will then drink to the bottom. Everybody joins in and drinks to the health of both families. The two men embrace, while the chief declares solemnly: "Cursed be the man who wishes the death of his neighbor."

The wife has no recourse to tribal law if her husband keeps a mistress outside of the home. But there are other effective ways. As soon as she has found out who the woman is, she calls her friends together, and they stand in wait along the path that leads to the well. When the adulteress comes to get water, they pounce upon her, tear her clothes, bite and beat her and throw previously brewed peppered water into her eyes. The culprit has no choice but to return to the village naked, followed by an ever-growing mob of women who ridicule and insult her. A very effective punishment.

Conclusion

There is a striking difference between the married life of the Baoulé and that of modern Europeans, Americans, or Moslems. For the Baoulé, sexual pleasure is secondary; fertility is what really matters. Procreation is religious, sacred. The act of procreation comes close to divinity, means communion with the fertility rites that rule the universe.

Sexual pleasure can thus be viewed as an obstacle that should even possibly be avoided so as not to lose sight of the most important aim, the chief desire: the child. Although there are no sexual prohibitions, parents react unfavorably toward children who "play in the sand," because they fear they might become *oulakafouè*. This untranslatable word means laziness caused by sexual debauch. The Baoulé is sure that a child addicted to sexual pleasure will lose interest in his family and in working in the fields; he will become a vagabond.

Another important thing to note is the permanent conflict between fertility and lineage. Family, in the Occident, means father, mother, and children.

Among the Baoulé it can include a hundred people or more, bound together for better or worse, so that a man will call his cousin "brother," his uncle "father," not as a figure of speech, but with the real meaning of close unity. Here, however, enters the equally potent counterforce of fertility. This cherished family and lineage must be perpetuated and extended. To do so, a stranger has to be introduced—as a wife or husband—to have children. Hence the drama of conjugal life: two forces in conflict, the battle between the cohesive pull of lineage and the desire for procreation. The two individuals are attracted to each other to extend their lineage, when at the same time each one is firmly held by his own lineage that will not yield. In this unequal battle, lineage always has the upper hand. There is never a rupture. Marriage is a temporary excursion, tolerated as such, from which each partner eventually returns to his lineage which had actually never let him leave.

Death

I. STANDARD FUNERAL RITES

As soon as a sick person has expired, his close relatives roll in the dust or mud and howl. When a child dies, his mother will have left him in the arms of a grandmother or aunt at the onset of agony so as not to see him die; she will go further away, throw herself to the ground half naked, and thrash around with her arms and legs.

One of the elders starts beating the drum with two special forked drumsticks in a syncopated rhythm. The sound is audible over a long distance. On a day when there was a funeral at Kouassiblekro I went to Brobo, ten miles away, and was able to hear the beat of the big drum all the way there. Everybody understands the meaning of that rhythm: the drums really speak. As soon as the villagers hear the news, they have to stop all work in the fields to participate in this great event—the departure of one of their people to the land of the ancestors.

For this event concerns not only the immediate family as in the west; it involves the whole village. All the notables go to the compound of the deceased. They try to quiet the relatives by holding their heads in their two hands, and speaking gently to them. Then the elders make the most urgent decisions. Who has to be notified? What type of funeral is appropriate to the position of the deceased? Who will organize the funeral dances? etc.

When these matters are settled, the corpse is carried behind the house to be washed. But before any water touches the body, the relics must be removed as they would lose all power once the body is washed. Hair, fingernails, toenails, and pubic hair are the relics that will be needed to determine the cause of this death.

The people who wash the corpse must hold a piece of wood in their mouth to avoid contagion. For the same reason, the water used will be poured into a hole dug for this purpose, and carefully covered. Then the corpse is rubbed with a special oil; the bodies of women are perfumed and painted with kaolin.

Exhibition of the Corpse

During this time, other women prepare the place where the corpse is to be exposed. The ground is swept and glazed with cow dung, the steps and the lower part of the walls are colored with red clay. A straw mat is spread on the ground, but it must be upside down; the surface usually used for sitting must face downward. (It is a bad portent for a living person who so forgets himself as to lie on the underside of a mat.) The corpse is placed upon a black-and-white cloth and covered with the number and quality of robes that befit his importance.

There is no special rule about the position of the corpse. If it happens to be a beautiful young girl, she may be placed upright upon a seat, leaning against a wall, her hands on her knees and her eyes open, so that people can once more contemplate her beauty and so that she herself can enjoy watching the dance held in her honor.

The people who washed the corpse are impure. A special lotion of kaolin mixed with water, herbs, and leaves is prepared with which they rub their bodies for purification.

Special preparations are made for the family who have to wear mourning. The brothers and children of the deceased rub their bodies with mud, the wives use red clay, the grandchildren kaolin. All close relatives cinch their waists with tree bark. Sometimes both men and women wear handbands; waistbands are worn only by women.

When everybody is ready, the chief gives permission to weep. However, if the death was sudden and the cause unknown, weeping is not permitted until the reason has been determined. When the signal is finally given, everybody raises one hand to his forehead (the Fafouè use the right hand, the Aari the left) and cries very loudly on a high pitch, improvising the words. The deceased is called by name. "Come and save me! I am lost, you have abandoned me. I have become an orphan. I am cold. I am thirsty, please draw water for me." The old women compose beautiful lamentations to praise the departed and express their grief.

The men sit on the ground, reserving the stools for the visitors. The women sit or even lie around the corpse to protect it, joined by one or two male relatives. If an animal—chicken, dog, goat—should touch the corpse or even get too close, it is immediately slain. For an important personage, a wide circle of cinders is drawn round the compound and any animal crossing it is killed.

Display of Treasures

Family and close friends bring their most valuable belongings, their finest robes, gold-topped canes and fly-chasers, gold jewels and head-bands, etc. They are exhibited near the corpse to honor the deceased while, at the same time, displaying personal wealth.

The chief is then asked to come. "Chief" [they may say], "our brother has died. We have prepared this exhibition to please him." The whole assembly then thanks the exhibitors with a special formula, "*nyakô, nyakô*," used only in funeral celebrations and never as an ordinary expression of thanks for gifts or services.

These objects remain exposed until the burial and are then recuperated by their owners. None of the valuable belongings of the deceased himself are shown except for the robes covering his body.

The Funeral Dance

The chief of the compound of the deceased sends young men for palm wine. They arrive at sunset, carrying earthenware jugs on their heads. This is the signal for the dance to begin; it must never start during daylight. Some men sit down in a large circle, with drums between their knees; they are joined by women who carry small sticks which they click together in a haunting rhythm (often quite disturbing to Occidentals). These sticks must never be used again after the funeral: they are cast away toward sunset.

The voice of a woman begins to chant: "Alas!

we can find nobody for this dance. We have organized a dance, and nobody will come to dance!" Little by little, a few women, then some men, enter the circle and dance. Everybody sings the couplet to the king of the birds. "Eagle! here is the game. Beautiful eagle, this is your game. Who will be able to play your game until the sun rises tomorrow morning?" Then the smoke rising from the brazier in the center of the yard will be asked to carry the message of woe to Heaven, the great divinity of the Baoulé. "Smoke, rise, go and tell Heaven that somebody has died here."

There will be couplet after couplet, sometimes traditional, sometimes improvised, until dawn or even until the next evening. And the dance may be repeated several times in the course of the weeks of mourning, sustained by palm wine provided by the family of the deceased. When I expressed my surprise, shared by other Europeans, about this joy shown at the time of mourning, one of the elders explained: "We are all mourning the death of our brother, and we suffer greatly. But the family should not be left alone to weep all night, so we try to distract them from their sorrow; that is why we play and dance for them." And it actually does happen that family members seem to forget their sorrow through participation in dance and song.

Rites of Divination

The most important part of the funeral ceremony is to find out who is responsible for this death.

There are seers who specialize in communication with the dead, but they are fairly rare. If they have to be brought in from a distance, this ceremony has to wait until after the actual burial. Here is where the relics of the deceased—his nails and hair—become important. The seer wears them on his head when consulting the auguries.

A bier is constructed from branches tied with vines. The relics are wrapped in white cloth and placed in the center of this litter. The seer and his aide carry it on their heads; the seer is always in front, as the aide has no powers of divination.

The crowd assembles in the yard or, if it is too small, in front of the village. Three men are charged with calling and exciting the spirit of the deceased; one carries a small bell without a clapper which he beats with a rod, the second a small drum, the third a wooden platter upon which he drums. These three instruments are sounded after every question asked by the seer. But before getting into the solemn adjurations, the deceased must be aroused from his stupor—from this indolence which caused him to accept his death without any reaction.

Provocation of the Dead

The assumption is that the dead man was murdered. He must therefore be torn away from his apathy and incited to vengeance, by making him denounce the culprit. To accomplish this, a man rushes from the crowd toward the stretcher brandishing a machete, and starts abusing the deceased with the worst of insults: "Cursed be your father! Cursed be your mother!" At that moment, the spirit of the deceased takes possession of the seer who goes into a trance and throws himself upon the man with the machete. They are forcibly separated, and some porters with the corpse move into the center of the circle with the litter on their heads.

Solemn Adjurations

Now begins the interrogation of the dead. The first question is of ancient tradition, invoking the great Baoulé divinities, Heaven and Earth. Never does a ceremony begin without pronouncing those two names. But here their invocation has a particularly solemn and mysterious meaning. Are Heaven and Earth, the great, the powerful, the ancient, coequal? Is not one of them greater, more powerful, more ancient? Which one comes first? Who is the chief? Supplications go to the dead person who has just passed into the Land of Truth to reveal this secret. To make this happen, two men are assigned, one to represent Heaven, the other Earth, and the spirit is asked who is the chief. The bier hesitates, leans first to one side then to the other, then stabilizes in the center, between the two. This agonizing question has been asked for centuries and will ever remain unanswered. There are always partisans of the superiority of Earth who claim that the relics leaned in the direction of Earth and had thus indicated her superiority. But the majority avows continued ignorance on the subject.

Then two men are secretly assigned the parts of Truth and Lie. The seer, who does not know who represents which, is supposed to bear down on Truth. If he leans toward Lie, the crowd disperses. It is considered useless to question any further, as either the seer is not up to the task, or the deceased does not want to tell the truth. If he chooses Truth, the trial can be repeated three times, with changed actors, to make sure that this experiment will be conclusive, and that the dead has decided to speak.

The questioners then try, by process of elimination, to find the cause of death. "Who killed you, Heaven or Earth?" Sometimes the litter firmly points to Earth; never will it indicate Heaven, for *Nyamya* has never killed anybody. Then all the minor divinities are reviewed. If no culprit has been found, the blame falls upon the defunct himself. "Did you violate one of the sexual taboos? Did you steal? Was it your theft that killed you?" If all replies are negative, there follows the worrisome question: "were you killed by an enemy?" An affirmative reply to this would strike terror into the assembly in former days, because it was inevitably followed by "who is he? show him to us and he shall follow you immediately to the land of the dead." And the supposed culprit was doomed to death without any further inquiry. It took a great deal of courage for those men and women to step up to the corpse and say, "If I am the one who caused your death, point to me." In our days this question is no longer asked, which takes much of the tragic point out of the ceremony. The Baoulé now merely request the defunct to kill the enemy responsible for his death, and not to leave him in their midst.

Finally, when the cause of death seems determined, the defunct is asked to indicate preventive remedies so that death will not return to the village, and to suggest the appropriate offerings, sacrifices, libations. But alas! despite all these measures, death will return for, as the proverb says, "There is no remedy against death."

At the end of the ceremony, the litter is cut into shreds and thrown toward sunset. The relics are buried near the grave of the defunct. The seer is paid. (In former days a chicken and a crock of palm wine would suffice, but the introduction of paper money has raised the price. I have been told of a seer of the Warebo people who demanded thirteen thousand CFA [about fifty dollars] for such a ceremony.)

Invitation to the Funeral

Even though the drums have been sounded through the village, the chief still sends the public crier to the village square to issue the official invitation to the funeral. In these invitations, it would be too crude to use the expression "dead." Rather, "he has been broken" (o asaki) is the delicate way always used to express the demise of a close relative or friend.

The villagers then go singly and in groups to the compound of the defunct to weep or sit in silence for hours, or talk quietly with neighbors. Absences are noticed. Sickness is the only acceptable excuse, for the whole village remains idle until the burial. However, strangers who happen to reside in the village must first go to the chief for permission to approach the corpse, as they might carry a bad omen, as do the animals.

There are, of course, villagers who are too far away to return, especially those who work in the coffee or cocoa plantations. When they do return, even months later, it is their duty to go and weep in every compound where a death occurred during their absence. This procession through the village, sometimes with many stops, is a tough assignment, particularly for the young who are not proficient in weeping, and are watched by everybody. They often try to arrive home late at night, and then team up with others the next day for these visits.

Reception of the Guests

The chief sends his emissaries to the other villages of the tribe with the news. All the roads and paths leading to the village are full of groups of men and women following their chiefs. The important chiefs are accompanied by their insignia: a buffalo horn and a drum, which is then called panther-drum because it devours the animals of the village. At the sound of this drum, the guests storm into the village and grab the first animal they see—ox, sheep, or goat—and kill it for their own benefit. Thus, to avoid this massacre, the chief who has issued the invitations sends somebody to meet his guests on the road; this emissary offers a chicken to the panther-drum, thereby appeasing his voracity.

The group enters the village in single file. First

come the women who enter the compound of the defunct in tears, and who then seat themselves around the corpse. Then come the men, also weeping; but they traverse the compound once, then march through the whole village in solemn procession, and return in the same order to the house of the defunct. This time, every man salutes the assembly with a majestic triple swing of his right arm —"*nyakô! nyakô! mo yakô!*"—and then takes his place on one of the numerous seats in the shade of a tree, not far from the compound. The women guests then also rise to greet the assembly.

Now it is up to the villagers to reply to the salutations of the guests. They do this one by one, in slow procession, with the same rhythmic arm gesture; then they sit down again. The chief now delegates one of his men to crouch before the guests to seek news of their village. After listening to the response, the host villagers again rise for another round of greeting their guests. This ritual is now reciprocated by the guests, who circle around the villagers, greeting them a second time.

At this point the chief delegates two of his people to go and "look at the stomach" of the villagers to find out whether they are ready to talk about the Broken One without reviving the pain too much. They return with the reassuring news that the villagers have bravely accepted the sad fact, and that it will be all right to present condolences. The guests thus rise once again to present their "*nyakô.*"

Moved by this gesture, the villagers now wish to present condolences to the guests. So the hosts, in turn, send two messengers to "look at the stomach"

115

of the guests, after which it is their turn to express their *"nyakô."* And it all ends with the palm wine which the villagers offer their guests.

To describe this ceremony is complicated and monotonous. There are actually no fewer than ten marches and four delegations, not to mention the repetitions, for messages and replies are never made directly to the chief, but rather transmitted through an intermediary. And everything is done in slow, majestic pomp.

Offerings

Before leaving, the guests have presented their offerings: money, mats, robes, animals. The objects are placed before the corpse, the animals given to the bereaved family.

There is a fixed schedule for these offerings. The spouse of the defunct should give a sheep, a blanket, or a robe. The mother-in-law gives Baoulé pants to her son-in-law and a cache-sex to her daughter-in-law. The other in-laws give a chicken. If the defunct were an important person, the family would give an ox.

The underlying principle for the choice of offerings is simply stated: "Funerals are the repayment of debts." If the defunct had not given generously to the funerals of others, he would get very little. Everybody therefore thinks of his own death and tries, in generosity, to prepare a glorious ceremony for his own future.

The gifts of mats, covers, and robes are used to adorn the corpse. The animals are killed, and used for food or for sacrifice. Money is a recent innovation, and is "accepted" by a person who does not belong to the family. After the funeral, he will give it to the heir who will use it as he wishes. But apart from this money, which is not in the tradition, no gifts are put to profane use. It is forbidden, for instance, to sell or even to keep an animal offered to the defunct.

Cemetery

Each village has one or more burial grounds. Sometimes one is reserved for the notables, the other for ordinary people; sometimes there are as many as there are quarters in the village. After the burial, the cemetery has no further significance; one does not go there to visit the dead. One may, however, go there for other reasons, to hunt, to cut wood, or such; children will even run through when looking for wild pineapples. The only two prohibitions are never to light a fire or to plant anything there. Anyway, villagers are apt to avoid it for fear of meeting ghosts, and there is no path or even trail that leads to this thicket.

When a villager dies, an elder goes to choose the place for his grave. Boys with machetes will go before him to cut a path through the vines and brambles, but he alone remembers the exact place where the others are buried. One must take great care not to expose bones; it would be a mortal sin, even if it happened by accident.

The zeal of the young volunteers who dig the grave is proportionate to the quantity of palm wine that they are offered. The richest families are apt to have the deepest graves. Hence the proverb, "When a poor man dies, the earth is hard; it is soft and fragrant for the rich." A notable may even get a more comfortable resting place: when the grave is deep enough, the workers will carve out a horizontal gallery or niche where the corpse can be laid, so that the soil will not fall directly upon the body.

Care is taken when digging to separate the layers of earth. Black topsoil goes to one side, the deeper red laterite to the other.

Presentation of Apologies

There is no rule about the time of the burial, but it seems that waiting until the day after the death is a sign of affection and consideration for the deceased. Sunset is the usual time to take the corpse to the cemetery, but there are exceptions. Corpses sometimes get decomposed quickly in the tropical heat, so the burial is done quickly and discreetly at night.

The most frequent reason for delay is the protocol of apologies. When an object of value is broken, somebody was responsible for the accident, and the object had an owner. Naturally the guilty party would present apologies to the owner, particularly if the damage is irreparable. The same holds true in death. Somebody was "broken" (*o asaki*), therefore the guilty—or at any rate those in whose care this person was—must beg the pardon of the other villagers whose cherished "possession" he was.

According to the proverb, "A man is worth a hundred times more than gold."

Burial

The chief-member of the family has slit the neck of a chicken and let the blood flow over the steps of the house. One of the wives of the defunct prepares a meal for him. She pounds the yams and cooks the chicken in his favorite sauce. Someone may warn, "Don't put in too much pepper; you know he didn't like that; salt it well, the way he would want it."

The men who specialize in burials are called *aloufouè*, and are usually attached to one family. They will have rubbed their bodies with charcoal and special plants which they know will protect them from the contagion of death, and they chew roots to protect their breath. The only fee they receive is a chicken that they will eat together after having discarded the neck.

They begin by making a bier from branches laced with vines. They then remove all compromising objects from the corpse, such as jewels, gold nuggets worn around neck or wrist, metal bracelets and rings, and especially those beads of mysterious origin called *nainglaiman*; for the sorcerers use those objects to inveigle the souls of the living. If one were to bury these things with the corpse, one would risk the death of other people. So serious a threat is this that an object forgotten on the corpse would be sufficient reason to lift the interdict and exhume the corpse.

The defunct is wrapped in beautiful clothes. These are the garments that he will present himself in upon arrival in the land of the dead, showing the ancestors how generous his family had been. If some close relative had not been able to arrive before the burial, a small piece is cut from each gift robe and presented to him, so as to show how much had been done for the deceased.

The *aloufouè* take a cloth and tear it into strips with which they tie everything into a straw mat; for neither corpse nor robes must be visible. The bands are then solidly attached to the bier, which is placed at the entrance of the compound.

The children of the defunct then come one by one, starting with the oldest, and stride over the body of their father or mother. They start at the right of the corpse; the boys do this three times, the girls four times; if there are babies, a grown-up stands on each side of the corpse and they are passed from one to the other.

This particular custom was explained this way: "It has often happened that children have soon followed their parents into death, which proves that the souls of children are bound to the souls of their parents. They must be detached from their parents so as to prevent their going together to the land of the dead. That is why this rite was introduced."

Very few villagers accompany the body to the cemetery. Women and children are not allowed, but not many men go either, be it from fear, sorrow, or disinclination. Even close relatives abstain. At the last funeral I attended, there were but seven at the grave.

First in the procession goes the man who carries

the two receptacles of food for the dead, one with mashed yams, the other with meat and sauce. The second man carries a pitcher of water; sometimes there is a third with a gourd of palm wine. Then, in no particular order, come the corpse and the other men. Two porters carry the bier on their heads, making sure that the body is always feet first. All the men take turns under the bier, for this is a way of giving pleasure to the dead. Everybody passing the procession on the way gives a coin with a wish for good luck.

Brambles make the approach to the cemetery slow and difficult; voices are lowered. The bier is placed at the edge of the grave. An elder examines the cavity with care, for it must be clear of any foreign element. The grave-diggers had removed all roots, leaves, living things. If therefore anything is now found in it, such as a twig, a mouse, a toad, it would be thrown far away, with care not to kill the animal; the people would then have to go back to the village and consult the seer about the omen attached to this thing before the corpse could finally be interred. This is a very dangerous moment, chosen by sorcerers to throw live souls into the grave who would then have to depart with the defunct to the land of the dead.

One or more straw mats are laid at the bottom of the grave, depending on the rank of the defunct; robes are never placed there, but are kept to cover the corpse. The *aloufouè* then untie the bier and swing it toward the setting sun.

An elder fills a goblet with palm wine, pours it into the grave, and invokes all ancestors: "Come, here is your wine, drink it and protect us and all the people of the village." Among the Pépressou and Fafouè, two *aloufouè* go down into the grave to place the food in a corner; then they receive the corpse into their arms and lay it at their feet. The Aari have very narrow graves, so the *aloufouè* kneel at the edge and gently let down the corpse with the bands that attached it to the bier.

Graves are always carefully oriented east-west. A man must be placed with his head to the west so that his eyes are turned toward sunrise; for his thoughts, they say, were always turned toward the rising sun which gave him the signal to leave for work in the fields. A woman's head is placed to the east, so that her eyes turn toward sunset; for her chief preoccupation was to start cooking dinner the minute the sun would set. Never is a corpse laid on his back, for reasons of comfort, but rather on one side. A man will lie on his right side, a woman on her left. For that is the customary position of married people: the husband always sleeps to the right, on his right side, the wife to the left.

Before covering him with earth, an elder approaches the defunct and bids him farewell in the name of the whole village, for this is the exact moment when his soul leaves for the land of the dead. If the rites of divination had not yet been held, a further plea is added: "Yao! we are now bidding you farewell; we do not know who killed you. If the Heavens have taken you, rest in peace; but if it was an enemy, kill him and take him with you to the land of the dead."

The first earth put down is the topsoil reserved for this purpose because it will cling to the corpse.

This earth, having been on the surface, has heard everything the villagers have said and has seen everything that has happened during the departed's lifetime. Now it will tell him the whole truth. The living can be deceived; but death clarifies everything—there is no more mystery for the dead.

One by one, everybody now straddles the grave, one foot on each side of the pit. In a slow, swaying motion, they drop a little earth alternately from the right and the left onto the corpse, raising both hands to heaven at each motion. This ritual is repeated three times for a man, four times for a woman. The raised hands look as though they were pushing something away. I am told that this is a gesture of exorcism, an attempt to chase away the bad fate that brought death to the village.

The grave is then filled up, and completed by a little slope that everybody treads down so as to make it firm. Here the Aari tribe places the food for the defunct. An elder makes little balls of yam dipped in sauce; turning slowly, he throws them over his shoulder toward the four cardinal points, invoking all the ancestors to come and eat. He repeats the same thing with some meat. He then places two dishes filled with yams and sauce onto the tomb next to the goblet of water.

To end the ceremony, everybody assembles around the grave, drinks what is left of the palm wine, and goes back to the village. At the edge of town, they light a fire in which they singe the tools used to dig the grave so as to purify them from contagion with death. For the same reason, everybody washes hands and feet in water with special herbs and leaves.

The Baoulé groups whose custom it is to place food inside the tomb will visit the grave two or three days after the funeral. A family member will get some palm wine and invite a few friends to accompany him to check the grave. When he sees that everything is all right, he pours a little wine onto the earth, calling out the name of the defunct. Then the friends sit down at a distance to drink the rest of the wine they have brought.

The Aari, however, who leave food outside the tomb, have a much more thorough system. They need to find out the wishes of the defunct: if he has eaten what they served him, everything is all right; but untouched dishes are manifest proof that the defunct is angry, and they have to know the reason. The seer has to be consulted, and he will question the defunct to find out the cause of his anger. He will then be appeased by offerings and sacrifices until the food has disappeared. I have been assured that only the defunct eats the meal that has been prepared for him; numerous tracks of dogs, rats, birds have been seen on the grave and the food has remained untouched; at other times the food has completely disappeared without a single trace of any animal or intruder.

Treasures

In former days there were enough gold nuggets and gold sand to be found in the sub-soil so that most old people these days still have a little personal hoard when they die. While this gold is not a real divinity, it still belongs to the ancestors, and the dead watch its disposal with interest.

To preserve this gold against fire or theft, it is put in an earthenware pot which is buried under the house or at the edge of the village, or sometimes even further away in the fields. The owner is the only one who knows the exact spot, and he will notice certain marks or places so as not to forget where it is.

While certain possessions of value such as statuettes or sculptures representing deities may pass to any one of the children, the pot of gold must go to the sole heir of the defunct, i.e., his younger brother or sister. If they are all dead, then, according to the matrilineal system, the oldest son of the youngest sister gets the heritage. According to the legend, Queen Pokou was the one who started this matrilineal system, because she sacrificed her son, the nephew of her brother, the king, to save her people at the crossing of the Comoë.

The heir is never told the location of the treasure so that he will not be tempted to possess it prematurely. Instead, the owner will reveal the secret to a trustworthy friend who will then inform the heir after the owner's demise. Upon receiving this information, the heir leads a sheep or even an ox to the indicated place, and sacrifices the animal to the defunct and to the family ancestors.

It can happen, however, that an overly cautious man waits to the last minute to reveal his secret; there are even some who refuse to speak at all. Family, friends, and particularly the heir himself will come to the bedside of the dying man and beseech him to tell somebody where his treasure is hidden. Be it from greed, spite, or because of an old grudge against his heir, the man may die with his secret. This gold is lost forever, for all search is in vain. They get even with the defunct, however, by giving him a very short funeral.

II. SPECIAL FUNERAL RITES

Kings and Chiefs

The death of a king must not be published. This catastrophe is proclaimed by the words "the king's feet hurt." Everybody understands that this means he is dead, but it is forbidden to speak of it or to weep. Every village sends two delegates to the court in formal visit; but instead of the usual condolence for deaths *"yakô,"* they will merely say *"aouyô,"* the word of regret for any other misfortune.

The Baoulé expresses the pain of death in images of cold, of chill. "Death has stiffened the corpse, and the family suffers from cold." "We sympathize with your chills" is said to people in mourning. So as to spare a king the pain of feeling cold when he is dead, he will be given companions to keep him warm. Slaves once were beheaded—four to twelve, depending on the importance of the king—and their heads used to be exposed upon the seats of the ancestors, beneath the eaves. It has been believed that the wives of the king were once offered as sacrifice for the defunct. This is wrong on two grounds. In the first place, the decapitated people were always strangers from the North who had been obtained during the Samorai wars. In the second place, it is wrong to speak here of human *sacrifice*, because words like "adore" and "sacrifice" are never used in this ceremony. The only term used is "keeping the king warm."

As soon as the king is dead, a grave is dug in his own compound. He is buried there in his ordinary clothes, and described as "leaning back." This is done in great secrecy. Not until one or sometimes two years later is the death of the king officially announced. On a given day, the *aloufouè* disinter the completely decomposed and desiccated corpse. The skeleton is then laid out under robes in the palace, and the complex funeral celebrations begin. They last for several months.

The place for the grave has been carefully selected by important officials. It must be distant, isolated, and situated near water. During the dry season, this poses no problem: the grave is dug in a dry pond or water course. During the rainy season, however, a dam has to be built to divert the water before the trench can be dug for the grave. At a certain depth, an "L"-shaped tunnel is made, the horizontal gallery leading to the sub-soil of the bank. Then, in the dark of the night, unbeknownst to anybody, the *aloufouè* deposit the skeleton. The entrance to this cave is closed off with heavy timber joists, covered with animal hides, then the vertical tunnel to the surface is entirely sealed. After that, the dam is destroyed so that the water flows as before, leaving no trace of the tomb.

In olden times, all this mystery and secrecy about the death and burial of kings was indispensable.

It was needed to prevent raids by enemies or foreigners who might have sought revenge by violating the tomb of a king.

The Three First-To-Die

In every family, the first three children to die are *féa*, which means that they have no right to a formal funeral. These first three are counted by mothers, not fathers. Say, for instance, Yao has two wives, Akissi and Aya; Akissi has five children, Aya has seven. There will be six *féa* in this family, i.e., the first three children to die of both Akissi and Aya. There is no exception to this rule. No matter how old or how prominent these people have become before they die, they still remain *féa* and can have no funeral.

Panic breaks out at the death of a *féa*, as his body must be disposed of as quickly as possible. Upon death, the corpse is immediately removed from the house, to be washed outside, which is done fast. Small balls of white cotton are then affixed to the body, which is tied into a straw mat, carried outside the village by two men and put under a tree while the grave is dug. The "wrapper" was sewn without any colored thread, only white could be used. Only two or three men are present, just enough to keep the animals away. This straw mat lying at the feet of hurried, preoccupied people looks like a bundle of merchandise carried by a travelling salesman who might tarry a minute on his way to the next village. If the *féa* dies in the fields, his body is not even permitted to reenter the village.

No sacrificial offering is made to earth or ancestors. Instead, somebody stands at the feet of the corpse holding a chicken, wrings its neck and brutally tears off its head. The chicken is rapidly grilled with a yam on an open fire, then halved lengthwise; the left half and the yam are deposited with the corpse instead of the usual food, though the Aari do add sauce to the chicken.

The grave is not in the cemetery, but where the village garbage is dumped. A banana leaf is placed at the bottom of the pit, the corpse is laid on it and covered with another banana leaf. The cavity is filled rapidly, the ground smoothed over, and that is all. The whole procedure is over in about an hour.

Back at the house, the father and mother of the defunct are washed with the same lotion usually prepared for those who have washed the corpse. It is then sprinkled over the house and the family, with the invocation "depart, *féa*." Father and mother are clad in white robes; the father will wear them for three days, the mother for four. Whatever the time of day, a meal is immediately prepared for the family which must be eaten, because fasting which is habitual for other deaths is forbidden for this one.

Tears are shed in silence—no weeping nor lamentations may be heard—to fall upon the food which everybody has a hard time swallowing. All the Baoulé agree that the death of a *féa* is by far the hardest for a family to bear. Formal funeral pomp offers somewhat of a compensation and diversion, and a day or two spent in contemplation of the departed is a comfort. Then there are the visits, offerings, dances that help one forget a little. For a *féa*, there is nothing at all, nothing but suffering in silence.

Why such a hard law? Not from malevolence, but from fear. With the traditional high incidence of mortality, it was important that the first three departures to the land of the dead pass unperceived. The ancestors who had convoked them would consider any noisy manifestation as a protest against their decision, and might respond by calling unto themselves the whole rest of the family.

Pregnant Women

A woman who dies during pregnancy, even if she is only in her third month, is called a "war casualty." For bearing children means going to war; when a woman goes to the bath house to give birth, she is told to be "courageous in combat," and after the delivery she will be told "you have come out victorious." To give birth means engaging in a battle for life against death. A laboring woman who is defeated by death is said to have fallen in battle.

Before this "victim" is laid in the grave, she is subjected to an operation by the *aloufouè*. Her abdomen is opened and the fetus is extracted; it is buried in a separate grave next to the mother's, so as not to violate one of the important tribal taboos which forbids burying two people in the same grave. The fetus, even at two months, is considered a person.

As for still-births or babies who live only a few hours, they are buried in the village garbage dump. But all other children, even babies a few months of age, are entitled to the same funeral rites as adults.

Sterile Women

Every woman who underwent initiation ceremonies and who dies without child is buried with
pieces of banana palm wood placed upon her barren
belly. As the banana palm is the symbol of fertility,
this should enable her to have many children in the
land of the dead. There is some variation in the type
of tree used, but the symbolic practice is the same in
all Baoulé sections.

Suicides

Suicide very rarely occurs among the Baoulé;
when it does, the person either cuts his throat or
hangs himself; it would be hard to determine whether
poisoning is ever self-inflicted.

If a person has hanged himself in the field, the
aloufouè go and cut the rope, then fell the tree, and
bury the corpse then and there, after having sacrificed
a goat to the earth. The same is done to a man who
has slit his own throat outside the village. In his case,
however, a grave offense has been committed to the
earth: spilling human blood on the land is a serious
crime, even in childbirth, and must be expiated with
sacrifices.

If a suicide was committed in the house, a hole
is knocked out of the back wall and the corpse passed
through it, so it will not cross the yard of the
compound. The house will then be left empty forever,
for suicide is a terrible malediction.

Lepers

Lepers are also passed through the wall after they die, but the hole is closed as soon as they are buried, and people go on living in the house: it is not cursed. A leper's corpse, however, is not taken to the cemetery; a large abandoned termite hill is selected and the corpse is buried in this vast cavity. In some regions, where this custom no longer exists, termite dirt is thrown on the body in the grave.

There is certainly no contempt implied in this extraordinary ritual, for lepers are loved and cared for as are all invalids. Their affliction is never mentioned by name; if one has to speak of it, the word *kaflè* is apologetically used so as not to humiliate them.

The termite represents the symbol of total poverty and dependence. "Heaven itself will draw water for a termite" says the proverb. Thus, this burial is meant to show the great compassion in which these cripples are held, taking the lead from the Creator who watches over the termite.

End of the Funeral

Generally the chief determines the end of funeral celebrations. That day, the heads of all the children of the deceased are shaved, "their heads are washed" in commemoration of the ancient custom which forbade all close relatives to wash during the whole period of the funeral. Then a sacrifice is made to the ancestors, the animal is eaten by the family, followed by a bumper of wine, and the funeral is over.

No so, however, for the widow or widower. For them, there are three further stages to go through, each one closed by a special ceremony.

III. RITES OF WIDOWHOOD

Purification

For the first six months after the death of the spouse, the following rules must be observed:

You can drink only freshly drawn water.

You must walk with your hands clasped behind your back.

You may eat only once a day, at sundown.

You must not sing.

You must never hit anyone, not even children or animals.

You must refrain from sexual intercourse and any physical contact, including handshakes.

You must wear a garment made of bark cloth.

You must weep at sunrise and sunset.

You may eat only freshly cooked food, and must clean your teeth before and after every meal to make sure that there is no morsel of the previous meal in your mouth.

At the end of this period, the widow or widower goes with a friend out to the field to weep for a little while. Back in the village, he or she is asked to hand over to the heir anything that belonged to the deceased spouse. Then come women—they must be old widows—to wash the widowed with a lotion of herbs, kaolin, and other things. They bring with them a sponge made of the crushed trunks of two banana trees with which they wash the survivor, and a bark cloth with which the widower or the widow can dry off. The old mourning garments are discarded; a widower receiving new Baoulé-pants, a widow a new cache-sex and a short white robe, about half the usual length. A white thread is tied around their wrists and calves, heads are shaved. The house and the people of the compound are sprinkled. The same spraying then takes place in the fields. In the yam patch, the *tokpo*, the main tool for farming, is put into the hand of the widow or widower. Then his hand is seized again, and placed upon the fruits of the earth. If the harvest is finished, he touches one yam, and that whole heap belongs to the women who washed him. If the yams are still in the earth, he touches one knoll to designate the row which will go to the women. More weeping at the return to the village.

The First Breakfast

During the second stage that lasts about another six months, the widow and widower may wash normally, but must continue to weep and to fast. They are quite recognizable in their small white robes, the threads encircling their wrists and legs, and especially the sponge that they received the day of purification, and that they have to wear on their heads as a symbol of their condition whenever they are not carrying a load.

At the end of this period—about a year since the death of the spouse—comes a ceremony that must take place "when the sun stands still," meaning about noon. Once again there is a change of clothing. The white robe and threads are removed, and a white cotton belt is placed around the waist. The widower then receives a bracelet and a beautiful, large, colorful robe. The widow is given a lovely necklace of gold nuggets, and a robe of the type worn on holidays.

An animal is then sacrificed in the name of the deceased, and cooked with yams. When the meal is ready, the widower is offered a spoonful of the food, which he must refuse; another bite is offered, and refused. For a widower, refusal is to be made three times, four times for a widow. Finally they are allowed to eat, and the fast is broken.

Remarriage

The duration of this third period depends upon the individual, but the rules are different for men and women.

A widower regains his freedom very quickly, as he still lives in his own compound. He can take a new wife as soon as he wants, but must conform to a certain ritual: the belt encircling his loins since the first meal must be broken. For this, he must pass a night with a woman whom he does not love, after which he bursts the belt and throws it into the bushes. Only then can he espouse the woman of his choice. That experimental night is required to find out whether the deceased will accept his remarriage: if the concubine does not die, the new wife will be all right. The Baoulé always choose strangers for this perilous experience.

The situation of the widow is a little different because she is still living with the family of her late husband. At the end of mourning, her parents-in-law take her back to her own parents and say: "As our son is broken, we are returning your daughter to you." The parents accept her, but after a few minutes of silence, the in-laws continue: "We thank you for having given us your daughter, we have always lived on good terms with her; it is Death who makes widows and who has broken everything; would you agree to give us back your daughter?" The parents can then accept or refuse the renewed departure of their daughter.

The woman may then take a new husband; but she too must break her belt in union with a stranger who serves as decoy. The new husband then offers a chicken to appease the jealousy of the deceased. Then the wife will move to her new spouse's parents' compound.

Religion

Heaven, the creator and great master, is by definition the first and highest power in the Baoulé religion. From personal observation it seems to me, however, that ancestor worship is really the primordial element in this religion.

The Ancestors

As beside the material world there subsists the world of spirits, genii, invisible forces of nature that duplicate it; so also, in the human world, there is the world of ancestors that gives it life and strength.

To illustrate this comparison: when the Baoulé speaks of rice he means two things, the plant, and the power hidden within this plant. The Baoulé adores rice. He will built a miniature hut under which he loosens the soil and plants a few grains of rice. And there, from time to time, he will come and sacrifice a chicken so as to ingratiate himself to this fetish. Eventually the rice takes root, sends up a sprout, a stalk, and later grains that ripen and fall; while the leaves dry, the new grains have taken root and the cycle begins again. For whom is this sacrifice meant: the grains, the leaves, the sprouts? No! For behind the stalk, the plant, the leaves that wilt, and beyond all the vegetation that will rot, there is the mysterious invisible power hidden in the rice that must make it grow, but that is also able to act upon the human world, to help or hinder man.

Life thus exists beside, behind, above this world of men who are born, grow up, and die. A mysterious world from which life comes and into which life goes. A reality that transcends the biological world and is impervious to death, for death is a biologic function. Beside these lives that begin and end like the leaves of rice, there is a real life, a hidden power held by the ancestors.

This mysterious world that duplicates ours is called *blolo* (from *bé blolo kè*: it is said, supposedly) because almost nothing is known of it. It is also called "the village of truth" in contrast to the village on earth, that world of pretense where one never gets to the bottom of things, where men live in lies and deceive each other. As soon as one enters this better world, truth is revealed, and one can no longer be deceived. In this world, closely united people live in a village where a council of elders makes all decisions, serenity reigns in family life, marriage, birth, and solid friendships are formed.

All life comes from this world: every baby born on earth comes from *blolo* and, after a longer or shorter stay in our world, goes back there. This world of the ancestors is thus not a world of the dead, it is the other world.

The Baoulé believe that the fetus in the mother's womb is joined, by the second or third month, by a companion called *wawé*; together, they are a whole person (*sna*). But this *wawé* can and does detach itself from the fetus, and takes trips into the landscape. It can thus happen that the *wawé* is away when the baby is born: the baby does not move or cry. To call him back, the mortar is bangled loudly with the pestle, or the baby is rubbed with the pulp of yam and the *wawé* is invoked: "Spirit of the baby, if you are in the field or at the brook, come back quickly." The baby sneezes: his "double" has returned.

The *wawé* lives in the body, but every so often it leaves. In moments of great anguish, for instance, the Baoulé will say "my *wawé* has left me"; when the misfortune has passed, he declares "my *wawé* has come back into me." When a person faints, they say "his *wawé* is not in him"; upon revival, he returns.

The day comes, however, when the *wawé* departs for good. His companion, the body, is then no longer called *ounain*, but *saka* (corpse), which means "his little one is no longer in him." The same word is used for an empty seed pod, hollow okra, or the empty shell of a peanut. The *wawé* has left, but he has not gone far, he hovers in the vicinity; he will not leave for the land of the ancestors until the moment when his companion, the body, is covered with earth.

Even so, it is not the *wawé* who goes into *blolo*. The double disappears as does the body that disintegrates in the earth, and it is something else that goes to the land of the ancestors: it is the individual itself, transformed, who becomes *oumya* (ancestor).

When the boy—whom we shall call Yao—was born, he came straight from the *blolo* and was given a body and a "double"; but until he gets to the age of reason, Yao remains what he had been there, a little ancestor, an *oumya ka*. During this whole period, he remains in contact with the other ancestors and talks to them. And when he dies he will become an ancestor again. But when I ask just who it is who goes to the *blolo*, the answer is: not the body, not the double, but Yao himself, the Yao who existed before he had either a body or a *wawé*. The proof is that the *wawé* could be devoured by a demon without harm to the person who will become an ancestor anyhow. The *wawé* is but a shadow; the same word is used for the shadow that accompanies me when I walk in the sun, or the image I reflect when leaning over the water of the fountain.

Man of this earth always stays in touch with his land of origin. He retains his personality, his basic character, which cannot be changed because it was formed by old influences in the land of the ancestors. And then there are friends, a spouse, brothers, who were left behind there and who must not be forgotten. Statuettes are ordered, made in the likeness of a mother, a spouse, a friend from the village of truth; and sacrifices are offered before these statuettes to appease the people who are waiting for us at the other side.

The Baoulé phrase used for the dead means "those who went before us" and indicates that we will all return to our land of origin. On the other hand, the wishes one makes for the dead give us no clue of their state. For a friend, one might say "may he rest in peace, and may he have only pretty termites to lick him." There is no special punishment that one wishes for an enemy: "Be gone with your demon, and never come back." There is, however, a severe punishment for really bad people. It seems the ancestors refuse them entry into the *blolo*; they want no disagreeable people in their village. That is why some people have to suffer so long before they can die; others do die, but their *wawé* are observed by the seers, wandering in search of rest. This is also the fate of all suicides, who are refused entrance in the village of the ancestors.

While there is no formal tribunal for new arrivals, they are put through a different sort of judgment. Each deceased is called before the council of the ancestors and queried for news from the earth, with particular emphasis upon the question of how he was treated by his companions during his life. His reply is his judgment: for on earth the good are rewarded, the evil are punished. That is why there is always some uneasiness after the departure of a deceased: "What will he tell the ancestors about us?" A succession of deaths in a family means vengeance by the ancestors; and an excellent report will bring good luck.

The ancestors hold our fate in their hands. They can produce good harvests, they can heal the sick, they can make sterile women fertile, they can increase the game for the hunter. Everything is in their power.

The *blolo* is not in a definite location. I never saw a gesture of direction when people speak of the land of the ancestors. Certainly it is not in the cemetery: we have seen how little enthusiasm there is about going there, and how graves are systematically abandoned. The dead, however, are everywhere, in the village, the compound, the fields; people talk to them, call them for help when needed, tell them everything. And there is hardly a Baoulé who has not at some time or other met a dead man with whom he was able to have a conversation.

All religious and social life is originated by the ancestors who intervene in every decision concerning village or family. A dead person, however, has to wait until after his official funeral before he becomes one of the *oumya*. Of course he is given the proper food for his journey, which may take up to a week, depending on the group. But the real worship begins upon return from the cemetery.

Adoration requires sacrifice. Blood must be spilled to establish the supremacy of a deity over life.

The ceremony begins by sprinkling water on the steps of the house, convoking all the family ancestors: "here is your water, come and drink, we are bringing you a sacrifice." No new ancestor is adored alone, all the others are invited. A chicken is then killed and the blood spilled upon a given place on the wall, which always remains the same; a few feathers are stuck into the coagulated blood. The ancestors' preferred sacrifices are oxen, sheep, goats, guinea fowl, chickens; they refuse any other animals. Monday (to use a Western calendar day) is the day consecrated to them, and sacrifices will always be made on that day.

If the defunct had been an important personage, his sacrifices will be offered not on the wall, but on a drum or a seat. The *klain kpli* and the *klain sin* are the two special drums for the great ancestors. They are beaten to sing their praise, to pronounce proverbs in their honor, and then an animal is slain upon the drumheads. The big drum can be more than six feet high and is a special object of worship, for it represents the life of the ancestors. When it is beaten, a large circle is drawn with ashes; people must bare their feet, and approach in silence. In the old times, if the man holding the drum should have the misfortune of letting it fall, his head was chopped off at once. These days, it is deemed necessary only to make a slight incision in the man's ear lobe so as to let some of his blood fall upon the drum.

The ceremonial chair also symbolizes former great chiefs. It is usually the one he had used during his lifetime to sit in judgment, but some groups prefer to carve a new one for the occasion. Upon this seat, on which often rests the cane of the deceased, the blood of the sacrifice is spilled. Often there is but one seat representing all the ancestors of the village, but sometimes there are many. This is also the altar upon which the blood of an ox is allowed to run for the inauguration of a new chief in the convocation of all the ancestors of the village and the entire people.

The world of the ancestors unifies the Baoulé to a solid, unshakable block. They are united in the knowledge that they all come from that same world, and are headed back to that same mysterious region. This unbroken circle, this single life that withstands all worldly accidents, this "always living together," is a force of incredible potency.

Faith in the ancestors saves the individual from anonymity, prevents his being crushed by the group. For here, immortality is personal, not generic as in India where all melt into the great whole. Here, every dead person retains his individuality. In adoring the ancestors, they are called upon by name, one after the other. And as everybody is destined to join the council of the ancestors, everybody is worthy of respect while on earth. A neglected invalid will get his revenge after his death. The sick, babies, even fools, are respected: for, it might be important to have friends in *blolo* if they go there before we do.

The Great Heaven

The great chief of Baoulé deities is *Nyamia*, the god of heaven. He is given various titles: chief, master, proprietor, but is never called father. Incomprehensible titles are used for him, possibly of Ashanti origin, that testify to the mystery of this inaccessible god.

He is an immaterial force. Nyamia does bear the name of the celestial arch, but is clearly distinct from the blue sky that we see above our heads. The visible sky represents and at the same time hides him. To explain this, the old Baoulé will draw a comparison to a statue: "When you adore a statue, you see the carved wood, but you do not see the spirit within; equally, you see the heavens, but nobody has ever seen him who is inside."

As nobody knows what shape this god has, it has never been possible to make an image of him; "we don't know what he looks like," they say. There is thus no symbol, no sculpture, no carving representing him. Occasionally one can find an object called *nyamia-ba*, or "little heavens," such as a small arc affixed to a thatched roof, but those are fetishes that have nothing to do with Nyamia save the name. There are also little mounds of earth and certain trees that are called nyamia because some groups use them as a place where they worship Nyamia. But they are not intended to represent him.

Nothing is known of the origin of this god, so he is given the name *Anangaman*. When did he begin to exist? We know nothing about him. He shares the title *Anangaman* with other beings, for example the sun, or the seasons; but they all change during the day or the time of year, whereas Nyamia alone remains immutable and has always been so. Nobody can have the slightest influence upon him. Whereas one can injure the earth and incite the fury of the genii, Nyamia alone remains impassive. And nobody can get a grip on him. To some degree, all other divinities are within the hands of man and can be influenced. Man can own land, symbolic objects, fetishes; they can be bought or inherited. Nyamia alone is beyond his reach.

There is no place where one can find this remote god; earth and other deities have a fixed place where they can be convoked. Nyamia does not respond to the call of man. He is everywhere, dominates everything, sees everything—including the thoughts of men. He is immense, and as impenetrable as the virgin forest. It is said that he used to speak in thunder, and the seers were able to interpret his voice; but men became perverted, and now there are no seers able to comprehend his mysterious language. His distance and his immensity cut him off from mankind. How to reach him? The Baoulé stretches desperately on tiptoe to tender his chicken in sacrifice. Master of everything, chief of everybody, Nyamia has too much to do, he is overburdened: how could he possibly look after my personal case? I am much more comfortable with my fetish—left to me by my father—who belongs to me, is always on my side, and whose sole purpose is to take care of me.

Nyamia is supposed to have created everything. But for a Baoulé two contradictory facts can be true at the same time; thus, according to him, the earth, the demons, and the spirits were not made by Nyamia.

There are three words in the Baoulé language to express creation: *bô*, as the blacksmith forges iron; *dyra*, when you hand down things in your possession; *yi* means mysteriously giving rise to something. This last expression is also used for all the incomprehensible products of white man—cars, airplanes—as the work of magicians. All three expressions are used for Nyamia the creator. But never is he said to have engendered, given birth to, begotten the world or man. These words are not used for him.

Nyamia created everything; once it was done, he leaves it alone. Thus, demons and genii are at liberty to harm mankind. Nyamia lets them do as they please without interference; he has retired into the solitude of his tower, far from the world which no longer interests him. Nobody needs to fear him. He did set up prohibitions, particularly regarding human relations, against such things as jealousy, or disrespect toward parents. But everybody knows that this easy-going king will not punish. His specialty is to be kind. to love mankind: the only thing that really offends him is contempt of a human being. Thus, sexual crimes offend Earth, not him; incest, adultery, relations in the bushes require a punitive sacrifice to Earth. But if adultery is committed in the presence of a spouse, for the purpose of humiliation, that is a crime against Nyamia.

By being kind, and loving mankind, Nyamia has

become almost a simpleton, incapable of the slightest harm. His name cannot even be used in oath. "I swear by Nyamia" or "May Nyamia strike me dead if . . ." make no sense, for everybody knows that this god has never killed anybody. The same is true of curses. Spirits and genii can be invoked and will use their terrible power. Nyamia, however, has never brought bad luck to anybody. He is not dangerous, nor virulent; he has no fire in him.

As this god is never angry, he does not have to be appeased as the others do by sacrifices or expiation. Instead, he is offered sacrifices of praise from time to time to thank him. After a good yam harvest, for instance, the seer may decide to call a general feast in honor of Nyamia. Everybody offers this sacrifice in his own compound; but if a person does not want to participate, he is free to abstain without any retribution.

"Sunday" was the habitual day of worship for Nyamia. Because that day was consecrated to him in some of the Baoulé groups before the arrival of White Man, nobody worked on that day. But in the time of forced labor (during colonialism) Sunday was the only day of freedom, so people got in the habit of tending their own fields on that day.

The worship of Nyamia begins with a libation of water. This is his preferred offering, as water is his specialty: it is he who gives it to man in the form of rain. As to animals, he likes sheep or chickens, but they must always be white. For the sacrifice, the Baoulé raises himself on his toes, stretches his arms toward heaven and says, with apology, "My arms cannot reach you, that is why I have spilled the blood upon the earth." Sometimes the chicken is thrown onto the roof of the house to come closer to heaven.

Moreover, every sacrifice to the ancestors, the genii or the spirits, is begun with an invocation of Nyamia, asking that it be accepted. And the ceremony ends with a plea to him to complete what may be missing in the worship.

If Nyamia is not honored by frequent ceremonies of worship, his name nevertheless is spoken all the time.

To thank a person, one says:
> "*I am asking Nyamia to thank you.*"
> "*May Nyamia preserve you.*"
> "*May Nyamia brighten your face.*"

After any successful achievement: "*Only with the help of Nyamia.*"

Praising an orator: "*Nyamia himself put the words in his mouth.*"

Recovery from illness: "*It was Nyamia who saved you.*"

When it rains, Nyamia is thanked.

Escape from danger: "*Nyamia is great.*"

Upon finding a lost object: "*Congratulations to Nyamia.*"

In all difficult situations his name is invoked.

Before starting a complicated task: "*Nyamia is with me.*"

When breaking the earth for a new field: "*Nyamia, please help me succeed in this work that I am beginning.*"

A farewell to a traveller: "*May Nyamia go with you! May Nyamia bring you back!*"

Before starting anything whatever, one must

always say *"If Nyamia is willing,"* or else
one might fail.

Our expression *"what a lucky coincidence"*
would best be rendered as *"This was
Nyamia's doing."*

Earth

Heaven and Earth are inseparable friends. An
old Baoulé explained the reason to me. "Every time
you open your eyes, you see Heaven and Earth at the
same time; they are as the bell and its clapper, one
cannot conceive of one without the other; they are
indispensable to each other, they exist for each
other."

It is assumed that they are equals, but it is not
really known; even the bier and the corpse at the
funeral interrogation have never been able to tell us
the truth on this subject. Some say that Anangaman
created Nyamia and Asyè (Earth) at the same time.
(It is impossible to categorize the Baoulé religion
according to western theological concepts: each exists
in its own cultural matrix.)

Some Baoulé consider Nyamia and Asyè a
couple. Nyamia would be the husband, as he is above
the earth and has a loud voice in his thunder, while
the earth is under him, fertilized by Nyamia's rain,
quiet and gentle as a woman.

But these are individual interpretations, and far
from unanimous. Language is no help either, because
in Baoulé there are no gender distinctions that might
make Nyamia a masculine noun and Asyè feminine.

The two divinities are almost always invoked together: before sacrifices, before drinking palm wine, before the hoe strikes the earth in the field, before settling in a new house. But Nyamia is always pronounced first.

There is a basic inequality between Nyamia and Asyè. Earth is a spirit (*amoin*) that one owns, whom one can bequeath to the heirs. Earth can be convoked to a meeting place in the compound, under the tree in the village, in the field. For that purpose, a symbolic miniature enclosure of a few inches in size, is constructed, and that is where the sacrifices are made. Game is laid there for a few minutes after the hunt before it is cooked. In contrast to Heaven, men can certainly do harm to Earth by violating certain prohibitions. Earth must then be appeased by sacrifices— the favorite offering being the goat— for she (or it) has a terrible temper (though not as bad as other spirits such as Dyè or Lapain whose tempers are even worse).

In contrast to beliefs common elsewhere, Earth is not the goddess of fertility. As we have already seen, the female sex organ has such a role among the Baoulé. It is not necessary, for instance, for a woman to sow the fields; often it will be a man who cuts the yam and plants it in the earth. There seems even to be an occasional incompatibility between woman and earth. Quite often violations of the earth's prohibitions are committed by women, and when Earth is then appeased by sacrifices outside of the compound, women do not have the right to attend.

Nevertheless, Earth is the great divinity throughout Baoulé country; the name of Earth is the

one most often spoken, for this is a powerful deity—
and nearer than Heaven.

The Genii of the Earth

The genii or spirits of the earth (*asyè ousou*)
can take on human form and be visible to anybody.
They like best "to reside" in clumps of bushes, to be
near brooks, or stay on wooded hillsides. The genii
live in groups in their own villages. They co-habitate,
they marry and reproduce. They are always ugly,
deformed, humpbacked; they have toes or claws
instead of fingers; sometimes they are one-armed, and
their hair drags on the ground; they can be dwarfs or
giants. They steal bananas and tapioca for food, and
even drink palm wine.

Among them there is, however, an occasional
pure spirit (*wawé*); with whom only the seers, when
in trance, can make contact and talk.

There are good genii who like people. When
you meet them they will ask for news from the
village, will offer you something to eat, and will invite
you to dance with them. Occasionally one of those
will want to come and live in a human village. A seer
one day came to a Baoulé and said: "I have met a
genie who likes you, is following you around, and
wishes to live with you; have a little statue made for
him, keep it in your house and adore it." And so a
sculptor carved one of those little masterpieces that
one can now admire in museums all over the world.

But why are these ugly creatures represented so
attractively? Because, say the Baoulé, when a baby is

151

born it will look like the statuette in the house. Masks are made in the likeness of *amoin* (see below) and are always horrible, so as to inspire terror. When you want to express your admiration of a pretty boy or girl, you may say "he looks just like a statuette"; a real insult is to tell somebody "you are as ugly as a mask."

These little statues are kept in a corner of the house, now sometimes covered with a cloth, as thieves are aware of their current high market value. Before them is a little earthenware bowl into which a little food is placed every evening. Very often a second statue will be acquired for company so that there will be a male and a female: they cannot live in bachelorhood. Occasionally one of the genii prefers to marry a human being; he or she will stay alone, but claim one night a week from the faithful human owner. All genii have a name, which is sometimes passed on to the next baby.

There are, however, bad genii, too, who refuse to come to the village, don't like people, don't follow them, don't possess them; their job is to do harm, to kill people. They have to be appeased by sacrifices brought to the hillside or the tree by the brook.

The "Amoin"

The *amoin*, popularly known as fetishes, are mysterious forces that can be rendered favorable by worship. They are pure spirits (*wawé*), thus invisible. They appear in dreams, and the seers can contemplate them at their leisure. "They are creatures of extraordinary beauty," they say, "there is nothing like them on earth."

They are a gift that was made to mankind by the genii. The way the story goes, a child while walking in the woods suddenly came upon a clearing where the genii had built their village. As it was starting to rain, the child picked up a fetish that was out on the square, and put it in the shelter of a house. The genii rewarded the child by giving him the fetish as a present. Since that day, the *amoin* have spread through the land of the humans.

But how had they arrived at the abode of the genii? Nobody knows. It is certain that they are not related to Nyamia. He did not create them, he has no influence over them, and they in turn do not seem to know him. On the other hand, they serve as intermediaries between the demon and mankind. They keep track of the movements of the demon, and they notify men of impending trouble, and protect them. The *amoin* are a valuable instrument for man but a double-edged one because of their difficult character and their proximity to the demon.

In the old days the *amoin* were good: with a little water and some palm wine they became excellent servants. But now they have become very demanding, and if they do not get everything they want, they become accomplices of the demon who enters into them to harm man.

The *amoin* are not friends of man. There is none of the emotional attachment between them that there is between genii and man. The *amoin* are feared, because they can kill or save, depending on what presents they are given. The power of the *amoin* varies with what he is given to eat. Thus *lokosué*, the bowl on the forked wood at the entrance of the house, is full of strength and good will toward us when filled with good things such as eggs, peanuts, etc., but if we leave it empty for a while, it becomes weak and passes to the camp of the demon to turn against us.

The relation of man to his *amoin* is not one of respect but more of ownership, and his prayers often sound like bargaining. "If you give me a good harvest, you shall have your goat." "I know I promised you a chicken for your help, but I don't have one right now, so here in the meanwhile is an egg." And when man is dissatisfied with the services rendered, he may threaten to drop this *amoin* and get another one. "Go and fetch your *amoin*" is an expression that shows the purely utilitarian relationship. If the *amoin* proves to be ineffective, he is threatened, insulted, and finally thrown into the bushes. And for one lost, there will be ten new ones to be found, for their number seems to increase all the time. The seers can discover new ones if need be.

The Demon

The demon can do only evil. While Nyamia is unable to do the least harm, even to punish, Baé is incapable of doing the slightest good. Nobody knows who he is or where he comes from, nobody can see him even in a dream, nobody can converse with him; only the seers, through mediation of the genii, can keep track of his movements.

Baé's main function is to devour the *wawé* of humans. When Baé catches a *wawé*, he puts him under a big stone or in the slit of a tree trunk. During that time the man without *wawé* remains inanimate until the prophet consults the augurs to find the remedy: a chicken must be given the demon so that he will release the *wawé*. But sometimes Baé simply eats him up, so then the man dies and goes to the ancestors without *wawé*. That can be done because, as we have seen, the *wawé* is not necessary to become *oumya*: a transformation produces this new being.

Demons are numerous, there is usually one in every family, not all of equal virulence. *Kouankouan*, their chief, is the most terrible; one can never get rid of him, whereas *Sipè* is easy to exorcise. They have the power to corrupt by inserting themselves into the best things; only Nyamia can never be influenced by Baé. They can, for instance, transform themselves into roots against which you stub your toe and from which you contract a serious disease; or they hide in a squirrel which will provoke the death of a child; they can take possession of the kindest spirits and make them accomplices in murdering humans. As they can do nothing without intermediaries, they must therefore take possession of men, turning them into sorcerers.

Sorcerers

There are no regular sorcerers, and nobody knows them. But a seer was once told by the genii, when he inquired for the cause of a certain calamity, that the woman who lived alone at the edge of the village was a witch. She is possessed by Baé, it said; she is bad, she does harm, she tries to kill. The sorcerer himself often does not know that he is possessed, he merely feels something inside him that pushes him toward evil, he thirsts for murder, he wants to devour souls as does Baé himself.

Sorcerers act in solitude; they are covert. At night they may dig a hole on the outskirts of the village and bury in it the tail of a rat, the quill of a porcupine, the tooth of a monkey, covered with leaves. Or they may place a cowrie shell at the entrance of a house, or some leaves on the path where a person is to pass. Chiefly they will get hold of certain objects that belong to their victim; they will steal a shoe, cut a piece of material from a robe, sometimes they even need a few drops of blood or a bit of human flesh. They can throw invisible arrows into a person's breast that will cause slow death if a seer does not come in time to discover and extract what look like fishhooks.

When a sorcerer is denounced by a seer, he is feared but not hated, because everybody knows that he cannot help doing evil; it is not his fault that he has been possessed by this evil force. His death is decided only as a last resort, when all other types of exorcism have been tried and have failed.

Exorcism

There are a number of ways to exorcise the demon. Sometimes one puts a firebrand in the hand of a sorcerer while saying "Depart with your demon."

The sorcerer thereupon goes in any direction he wants, and returns later alone; the demon has left with the firebrand. Fire is the symbol of evil, of hatred, while cool water means happiness; "cool medicine" is the expression for the many aspersions used to chase away adversity.

To exorcise the family *baé*, the chief of the compound will go to the end of the village carrying a live chicken, revolve seven times, and throw the chicken into the brush. This bird held responsible for the curse will err until it perishes or is devoured by a wild animal. If anybody had the audacity to eat this chicken, he would be possessed by the *baé*.

When there is a calamity that affects the whole village, a general exorcism is declared. At cock's crow all the women go to the bathhouse and anoint themselves with kaolin. The grown women then cut branches of a certain tree which they carry on their shoulders. Two balls of half-pound yams (*foliè*) have been prepared, one white, one colored red with palm oil. Everybody files through the village seven times, dancing and singing, led by an old woman who carries the *foliè*. From time to time she throws a morsel outside the village and cries "Go away, horrid demon." The girls dip their hands into the bowls of water they are carrying on their heads, and throw it in the same direction, so as to quench the fire of the *baé*.

Then everybody assembles on the village square. Every woman has brought a whole yam which is deposited on a heap there, to be devoured by the animals or to rot: this is the food for the *baé*. At the end of the village, by the edge of the road, a good meal is prepared for the demon that should last him for a very long trip: two eggs are placed neatly upon leaves with an ear of corn and a whole chicken, killed but not plucked.

In the meantime, the women have gone to their compounds for a thorough cleaning. They pick up everything that is broken, spoiled, or of no further use, such as cracked pots, old brooms, broken stools, and pile them all on a heap outside the village. Then all the old water is emptied and fresh water is drawn.

This house-cleaning shows how cleanliness is connected with happiness. Misfortune, misery, mourning are symbolized by dirt. A man who is unhappy or sick is said to be "in dirt." Widows and widowers are washed to signify the end of mourning. Happiness is clarity, purity. "There is beauty on his brow" means that he is a lucky man. Worry and sorrow are expressed by uncleanliness. White is the color of joy, of happiness. (The Baoulé describe Europeans not as "white" but as "red," and all the statuettes representing Europeans have red faces.) The best wish is to say "May Heaven make your face very light." Heaven itself is very light inside. People wash all the time to purify themselves, people and things are sprinkled, white is used everywhere: cere-monial robes, kaolin body paint for dancing, white cotton on the corpse of the *féa*, all in quest of happiness that in olden days was synonymous with generosity.

The Prophet

The prophet has the privilege of the no-man's-land that separates the world of man from the world of gods. He can serve as the intermediary of several deities, but ordinarily specializes for one of them, either Ngbla or Komya.

Any man or woman can become a prophet; the function is not hereditary. A village usually has several prophets. Prerequisites are: excellent health to perform the exhausting dances; excellent memory and verbal facility to transmit the messages of the gods which often require extraordinary volubility; a strong and pleasant voice to speak and sing for long hours, sometimes all night. And finally one needs great perseverance to learn the minute details of the complicated ritual, and to remain faithful to the innumerable taboos imposed upon a prophet.

The novice serves an apprenticeship with an old prophet who teaches him the system of the augurs, invocations, dances, chants. This takes at least seven years, and even after the novice enters his new job his master accompanies him and watches him for some time.

The day of consecration finally arrives. A concoction of special leaves and water is poured over the candidate's head after his face had been washed in it. Then other leaves are crushed and the juice poured into his eyes so that he will become a seer. His whole body is finally painted with kaolin. He is reminded of all the prohibitions to which he will be subjected, and presented with his instruments: a statuette upon which a chicken is slaughtered, and a cow's tail into which "medication" is inserted. Only then can he speak in the name of the gods.

What is the prophet's function? First of all, he is the seer. He alone can transmit the oracles of the divinities. Quite possibly an ordinary person can be obsessed by a spirit, but the words he pronounces will be incomprehensible. The prophet is then called to explain everything. The prophet can communicate with the gods in five ways: the dream, the nine leather thongs that he plays on the sheepskin, the dance, the box with mice, the gourd filled with water, and kaolin. Each of these rites require more complicated explanations than can be given here.

The prophet is also the one who uncovers the evil schemes that the demon is secretly preparing, and who devises the means to negate them. And, finally, he is the healer. He specializes in the use of plants, and primarily exercises an extraordinary psychological influence that produces near miraculous healing of many sick people.

That is the limit of his power. He has no political power in the village. He can give advice to the chief and to the villagers, but they are free to disregard his counsel, and to proceed at their own risk.

Liturgy

The Baoulé have no liturgical calendar, and there are no fixed holidays during the year. The Agni still have the feast of the first fruits when the yams are ready for harvest, but in the Baoulé provinces this celebration has all but disappeared, remaining as a ceremony only in a few families. Village celebrations are called for specific occasions such as funerals and epidemics, or upon decision of the chief or the prophet.

Suppose a crime were committed against Earth:

two men have started a fight in the field, they have hit each other, and blood has been shed—all a grave offense to Earth. The two men, now ashamed, return to the village without telling the story.

Shortly thereafter the son of one of them falls ill. All sorts of offerings are made, to no avail. The father finally gives in and goes to consult the prophet. Clad in his liturgical garb—white robe, head-dress of cowrie shells, bracelets on his arms, anklets on his legs, a cowtail in his hand—the prophet goes to the village square to dance. He begins by slowly repeated invocations of his spirit Ngbla; the rhythm gradually accelerates until his whole body shakes, the jewels clang, and suddenly he starts turning at a giddy pace: Ngbla has seized him and is getting ready to reveal the secret to him.

Gradually the prophet recovers. His *wawé* has come back from afar, where he was visiting the gods. At this point the prophet pronounces the oracle: there has been a fight between two men, blood was spilled, Earth is taking revenge by killing the child; to save it, a goat must be sacrificed to Earth in expiation.

The next morning, Wednesday, the day consecrated to Earth, the whole village is convoked. Everybody washes, rubs his body with kaolin, and proceeds in single file to the field where the crime was committed.

The first thing to do is to call the spirit who may have gone far away. This is the job of the *akotô* (acolytes who accompany travelling kings and sing their praise). Here they are told to raise their voices very loudly so as to be heard by the gods. "Asyè!

Come quickly, we are bringing you a sacrifice." Then they sound their musical instruments—drums, bells, gourds with cowries—as the spirits are susceptible to music, are easily charmed by the sounds, and respond to the call.

The *akotô* intensify the expression of praise: "Earth! you are immense; Earth, you are bountiful," then quickly change to insults, because the most effective way to waken a sleeping spirit is to revile him: "Mean spirit! horrible spirit!" Finally the prophet, who has even resorted to throwing two eggs into the distance to attract this vagabond deity, announces that Earth is now present and ready to listen to the prayers of the faithful.

The owner of the land—whose spirit Asyè is—goes to fetch water from the nearest brook and pours some onto the place where the crime happened, with the prayer "Earth! accept this water and drink it; and please listen attentively to what we are going to tell you."

The two culprits then prostrate themselves and make public confession. If they do not speak distinctly enough, they are told to raise their voices so that the spirit can hear them. With their right hand clasped in the palm of the left, they supplicate Earth to forget their transgression: "Forgive me, I am but a child and not very intelligent, my head is at your feet." Then they rub their lips on the earth several times and say "I will never do it again, never, never; my mouth is in the ashes, the ashes."

Now the sacrifice can be made. At this point the priest comes in, "he who stands up before the spirit." Each spirit has his priest who is the only person qualified to make the sacrifice. But, first, Earth's inclination must be tested. Will she be willing to accept the goat that the culprits have brought as a sacrifice? To find out, the priest will kill a chicken, cut it open, and examine its entrails: if the sex organs are white, it means that the spirit is willing; if they are black, Earth has refused. In that case, the experiment must be repeated with another chicken until the sacrifice is finally approved.

The priest then seizes the knife and cuts the goat's throat while saying "Earth! receive this goat; eat it and be appeased," or a similar prayer. In Baoulé liturgy prayers have no memorized wording but are composed for the occasion. Not many priests pray well. Some say too little and are at a loss for words; others engage in interminable tirades that wear out the assembly. Those who find the perfect balance are greatly admired.

The villagers cut up the slaughtered animal while others light the fire and set up stakes to grill the meat. The smell of the smoke brings anticipation and cheer to everybody. Tongues are loosened, people start to chat and to laugh and warm conviviality spreads among everybody. All feel united when the meat is passed, united and strong in their spirit of Earth. Hatred subsides, the culprits are reconciled. If, however, two other villagers had the misfortune of getting into a fight on the way home, the whole sacrifice would be spoiled, and would have to be undertaken all over again, which goes to show that the main purpose of the ceremony is the unification of the faithful around the divinity. A sacrifice is designed to quench not only the flame of anger and hatred that burns in the deity, but also in the hearts of men.

There is another ritual that pleases the divinities as much as sacrificial blood, and that is the dance. The rhythm of voice and body movement appeases and charms them; no god can resist the seduction of a beautiful dance. The dance for Dyè is a good example.

Dyè is a deity for men. Women cannot look at him, under pain of death. His worship is organized by a brotherhood. A group of men—about thirty—will decide to bring this god into the village. After asking permission of the chief, they have a mask made which they place in a small hut at the entrance of the village.

In the event of a calamity such as a smallpox epidemic, the men will decide to dance Dyè to obtain his aid. The brotherhood, headed by a priest, convokes all the men of the village to the sanctuary. One of them gets out the hideous mask with its large protruding teeth and places it in front of the hut; the little boys tremble with fear but cannot resist the meal and the dance that will follow.

The *akotô* call Dyè by blowing syncopated sounds in a buffalo horn. As he did not expect this visit, it takes him a long time to come, but the seer finally sees him arrive.

The priest lowers his Baoulé-pants a little to show that he is a man, then puts his index finger into his left ear, fills his mouth with palm wine, and spits it violently onto the mask. The care-taker of Dyè steps forward and offers a libation of water to

Nyamia, Asyé, the Oumya, and Dyè: "Here is your water, come all and drink it."

The priest then breaks two eggs on the mask and rubs them into its muzzle. Then he kills a chicken or a dog and lets the blood flow over the head of Dyè. The animal is roasted and everybody gets his share in a special ritual: each man steps up behind the priest who serves the morsels of meat to him over his shoulders; it is easy to play a trick and come by twice for double portions. Slices are put aside for the absent and the sick and are taken to the village later on, so that all men can participate in the sacrifice.

Then comes the main part of the cult of Dyè: the dance. A man covers himself with raffia and puts the mask upon his head; at that moment he as a person has ceased to exist, nobody can call him by name, he has vanished and has become Dyè. The dance goes on all night and even part of the next day, all through the village, the mask marking the rhythm, always well surrounded by others. All women are locked in their houses, but the dance stops at certain times to allow them to go to the well for water; as soon as they are back home, the fanatical round continues with its fiendish sounds and piercing cries.

From time to time Dyè emits an oracle. The prophet puts his ear close to the muzzle of the mask and translates the raucous sounds that are incomprehensible to the dancers. Dyè, charmed by the dancers, decides to save the village from the terrible epidemic.

The Sweet and the Bitter

The Baoulé are almost always smiling and relaxed. For a long time I would ask myself what was the source of their happiness. After all, the village is riddled with misery: hunger, disease, fear of the supernatural, death. They are at the mercy of drought, fire, angry deities. If their child is afflicted by a serious disease, they can do nothing but wait for death. Despite all this, there is always joy in the village: bursts of laughter from the young people on the square, the smile of the old woman spinning her cotton, the song of the man who swings his machete in the bush as though he were dancing. Suffice to listen to the women chatting in the moonlight at the time between harvests when there is not much left to eat. Instead of complaining, they tease each other with peals of laughter. "Did you cook a good dinner tonight? No? I didn't either. We must all have forgotten how to cook!" When you think of the tense, sad faces of the women you see in the streets of our big western cities, you may well ask yourself where happiness is, what makes life "sweet": for that is the term used to express the joy of living.

For the Baoulé, "sweetness is in your mouth"; that means that there is no abstract "good" in the future, nothing conceived or imagined for which you strive or to which you run. Happiness, the good, is something experienced here and now, something lived and tasted. Fruit that is not yet in your mouth or that is no longer there, is not "sweet." To understand that, one needs a concept of time quite different from ours.

For an Occidental, time is a possession; it is something separate and distinct from us, it is outside of us; "time is money" shows this attitude clearly, as do other common expressions: to have time, put time aside, save time, not waste time, use time well, lose time. Our happiness is firmly tied to the time at our disposal; leisure time, vacations, time to do what we like.

The distinction of three different times—past, present, future—is very important to us, and we value all of them, with possible preference of past and future over the present. What was in the past becomes a possession, well illustrated in French, where one says "I *have* 30 years," meaning that thirty years of experience belong to me. And we live continually in the future with our projects, programs, prognostications, due dates. Straddling these three times, we are pulled here and there, preoccupied, rushed. Happiness is for our future, we prepare for it every day, but it is never for today. A young person works to get a job; grown, he works to get a house or to prepare for retirement in old age. And Western Christianity caps it by stating that one must live in faith and hope, meaning that happiness is not for this world but only in the hereafter.

For the Baoulé, time is not a possession, not something that one has, but rather something that adheres to us, something that we live. And in that sense, the Baoulé never lacks time, since time is a part of him; he needs only to live fully in every moment of the present.

This hiatus in our two cultures became painfully obvious to me one morning when we were going to pick cotton. My neighbor had asked me the night before whether I would help him, so I was there, at his door, when in comes one of his cousins for a visit. So we sit down and we gossip for a long, long time. My friend is calm, relaxed, and lends himself completely to his guest: for time belongs to everybody, it is communal. As for me, I fidget, I cannot listen to the conversation, my thoughts are not there but in the field. I think of the cotton that will be lost because of the impending rain. I even think ahead to the month of October, when my friend will not be able to send his son to school because he will not have the needed money.

In Baoulé country, the only important thing is the present. The past as a quantity has no importance, only untimely events make a mark on memory. "How old are you?—I don't know"; not only from ignorance, but from lack of interest. I have often tried to tell parents the age of their children; by the next day, they have forgotten. "How long did it take you to work that field?—Since when have you been sick?"—such questions remain unanswered.

Future does not exist. When I am sick, I think of how I suffered last night, and I already see myself on that sickbed for days and months to come: the past and the future increase my suffering. The Baoulé, on his mat, suffers less because he has only the pain of this minute to bear. He also enjoys the present minute, and enjoys it more. At harvest time, he eats his yams in complete bliss, not thinking of the days of scarcity that will come. Our vacations are poisoned by the date of return to work which never leaves our mind. We do, of course, avoid some troubles and prepare some pleasures by our foresight. But looking ahead does, in itself, spoil a part of our present happiness.

"You, white man, are forever calculating, your heart is never calm" they say to me. They will go to the forest to cut stakes to build a house; when they return, they notice they are lacking a dozen or so. So they have to go back. They are in fine form, happy as can be, the women sing and clap their hands. They will make mounds until nightfall without counting how many yams they actually have to plant in this field; not until the next morning do they see that they have made a hundred more than needed: wasted work. As for me, I am forever thinking ahead, I count everything minutely, I measure, I calculate, and thus my work is efficient. No waste of energy, no waste of time. But I am always tense, and thus less happy and less open to others, less affable. "Your face is bitter," they say.

By this same token, the absolute, the definite does not exist. "Anangaman" which is forever—in the past, present and future—is not within the human realm. For the Baoulé, all is relative, even their religion. Their form of animism is something that works today, but if one were to find something more effective tomorrow, they would try it. My genie protects me perfectly at this moment, but I have made no agreement with him, so if one day I am not satisfied with him, I will throw his statuette away.

The inflexibility of Europeans is a source of mystery to the Baoulé. Once a white man makes a decision, he will not change it, the matter is settled once and for all. Any entreaty to postpone his departure, to lower his price is in vain. The decision of a Baoulé is made for the present moment: he settles a time to leave for Abidjan, his bags are packed, farewells are over, when something intervenes or somebody begs him not to leave. He will abandon his trip with the greatest ease, and have as good a day as ever. Whereas I, the European, would be completely upset by such a change of plans, and it would take me hours to recover. We are bewildered by the potency of the *yaki*, the supplication. After long and earnest deliberations, the elders can have formed a verdict: yet it takes only the petition of a mediator to modify the decision. The hardest, toughest Baoulé will melt when an old man bows down to clasp his knees in supplication.

* * *

But today, where is this sweetness? Times have changed. A long time ago, when the Baoulé came from Ghana, they invented the genii, the fetishes, the mysterious spirits that save. Two centuries of experience have led to this conclusion: "Our fetishes can no longer save us. White man has a fetish much stronger than ours: Money." Money seems as mysterious a force as any other fetish. "We don't know where it comes from or what it is; the paper of this money is cut by white man." With money one can get anything. Money is sweet. You must "have" as much as possible to be happy. In olden days, the important thing was to "be together," regardless of what one had; one could be happy with empty pockets. Now it is essential to "have," no matter what one is or becomes.

In the quest for political and economic independence, cultural independence has been abandoned, forgotten.

Biographical Notes

VINCENT GUERRY is a Benedictine monk of the monastery of Bouaké, Ivory Coast. He has chosen life among the Baoulé as his vocation. He does not proselytize, preach, or try to convert. He lives humbly and simply in this African village. He rises at dawn with the men of the village, wears the same clothes, works with them in the fields; he eats the same food, and chats with them in the evenings on the stoop or under the big tree on the square.

Father Vincent had lived and worked this way for about seven years before his friends persuaded him to write down what he considers a beautiful way of life, so that more people could get to know and appreciate it. Though this account is necessarily that of an outsider—aware of other values—he has penetrated deeply into the culture in which he still lives.

The translator, Nora Wärndorfer Hodges, was born in imperial Vienna, where it was normal to be fluent in at least three languages. Married to Professor Charles Hodges, author and professor of international politics at New York University, she was a teacher at the Dalton School in New York for thirty years.

When her husband died, she "retired" into the Peace Corps, serving as a volunteer in Tunisia for two years before becoming director of educational programs in the Ivory Coast. It was in this capacity that she "discovered" *La Vie quotidienne dans un village Baoulé*, which turned out to be so sympathetic an introduction to West Africa that she decided to translate it into English.

Three Continents Press titles in this SMALL-PAPER series:

Beside the Fire (Two Igbo stories from Nigeria) – Obioma Eligwe
Ghana: Fresh Views by Ghanaians (essays on history, politics, etc.)
The Prophet and the Warrior: Two Zimbabwens' Approach to European Invasion – Solomon M. Mutswairo
Life With the Baoulé (Ivory Coast) – Vincent Guerry, translated by Nora Hodges.

ISBN: 0-914478-15-X (Casebound)
ISBN: 0-914478-16-8 (Paperback)

Three Continents Press • 4201 Cathedral Ave., N.W.
Washington, D.C. 20016